GEORGE KENNEDY ALLEN BELL, Anglican Bishop of Chichester from 1929 to 1958, is revered nationally and internationally as a pioneer of the ecumenical movement and a peacemaker. Forming a bond with theologian Dietrich Bonhoeffer, he assisted the resistance to Hitler, aided refugees and supported imprisoned conscientious objectors, and courageously opposed indiscriminate area bombing as a war crime.

Bell is celebrated in the Church of England calendar on 3 October every year, the anniversary of his death. But in 2015 his reputation was ruined overnight by a single posthumous allegation of abuse over 60 years earlier. The allegation was initially upheld by the Church, without proper investigation and with no opportunity for a defence. It was based on the civil law conclusion 'balance of probabilities' in a case that never went to court. Following further thorough investigation, the Church finally acknowledged its serious failings in handling the affair, but full restitution of Bell's name is yet to be achieved.

With a thoughtful introduction to the global importance of Bell's legacy by renowned scholar Keith Clements, this book is based on Ruth Hildebrandt Grayson's collection of letters and articles (both published and unpublished) written in the course of the campaign for justice and the clearing of the late bishop's name. It attempts to make sense of this sorry saga by placing it in the context other historical cases, contemporary trends and well-publicised flaws in handling of abuse within the Church.

Historian **Ruth Hildebrandt Grayson** is the older daughter of Franz Hildebrandt, a close friend of the late Bishop George Bell. Her family, together with many others, owes its existence to Bell's lifesaving work with and for refugees from Nazism during the Second World War.

Presumption of Guilt
The Church's Flawed Case Against
Bishop George Bell

Ruth Grayson's penetrating and perceptive analysis of the Bishop George Bell affair is a remarkable story of tenacity and integrity. This is a forensically astute and gripping account of one of the most egregious and scandalous travesties in the Church of England's safeguarding processes in modern times. Grayson's book reaffirms the complete vindication of Bishop Bell, while also holding up a mirror to the shoddiness, hubris and coverups at work in the current hierarchy of the Church of England.

– Rev Professor Martyn Percy, Aberdeen

In this valuable book, Ruth Grayson sets out many of the dimensions of what became a significant public controversy lasting several years. Altogether, her study yields a severe judgement of what the Church of England has become in a later age.

– Professor Andrew Chandler, biographer

It is stirring to be reminded of the link back to Bonhoeffer, Niemöller, and the Confessing Church and it is hard not to wonder what they would have made of the rush to judgement and defenestration of George Bell and his reputation.

– Lord David Alton, who delivered the 2023 Bell Lecture

The rush to judgement on the basis of presumption rather than evidence is one aspect of the continuing failure of the Church of England to handle cases of sexual abuse justly and with due process. The Bishop Bell case is a prime example, as Ruth Hildebrandt Grayson argues in this book.

– Janet Fife, co-editor of *Letters to a Broken Church*

Presumption of Guilt
The Church's Flawed Case Against Bishop George Bell

by
Ruth Hildebrandt Grayson

with an introduction by
Keith Clements

*In memory of old friendships,
and in gratitude for new ones*

First published in June 2025

Ekklesia Publishing
Edinburgh
Scotland
www.ekklesiapublishing.co.uk

Copyright © Ruth Hildebrandt Grayson. Introduction © Keith Clements.

Cover image © US Library of Congress, publicly icensed

The right of Ruth Hildebrandt Grayson to be identified as the author and creator of this work is asserted in accordance with Section 77 of the Copyright, Designs and Patents Act 1998.

Photographs and images are used with permission or license and are the copyright of their creators.

Production and design: Bob Carling
Editorial: Simon Barrow
Photograph: Bildagentur, Berlin

ISBN: 978-1-7397551-1-9

A Catalogue record for this book is available from the British Library

Contents

PUBLISHER'S PREFACE ix

ACKNOWLEDGEMENTS xi

PREFACE xv

INTRODUCTION
A Prophet With Honour: Who Was George Bell and Why
Does He Matter? 1
   Background and History 2
   Bell and Bonhoeffer 3
   The German Resistance 6
   The Area Bombing 7
   The Post-War Future of Europe and the Churches 8
   Continuing in Prophetic Ecumenical Mode 9
   'I Seek My Brethren': Further Reflections 10
   Why Keep His Memory Alive Now? 12
   Why it is Important to Set the Record Straight 14

CHAPTER ONE
In the Beginning… 17

CHAPTER TWO
'Balance of Probabilities' 23

CHAPTER THREE
The Context: Surge of Suspicion 27

CHAPTER FOUR
Case? What Case? 33
   Not a Court of Law 33
   The Reputation Trap 36
   Lack of Evidence = Evidence 38

    Believing the Complainant   40

CHAPTER FIVE
From Incredulity ... To Fury   43
    The Carlile Report   43
    Further Allegations and the Briden Report   46
    Guilty by Allegation   49

CHAPTER SIX
Rocky Road to Restitution   53
    An Epidemic of Ambivalence   53
    Continuing the Campaign   56
    At last! Light at the End of the Tunnel   59
    But Not the End of the Road   62
    The George Bell House Saga   63

CONCLUSION   69

ABOUT THE AUTHOR   77

PUBLISHER'S PREFACE

It is an honour for Ekklesia Publishing to be making this important book by Ruth Hildebrandt Grayson available to a wider readership for the first time. What you have in your hands is a revised and expanded version of a text that was privately distributed at an earlier stage in the Bishop George Bell case. This is a saga which, as *Presumption of Guilt* explains, is not entirely resolved, but which has moved in a clear direction following the kind of detailed investigation which should have been its hallmark from the outset, but was not.

Why does this matter? For several reasons. First, as Keith Clements explains in his fine introduction to the life and work of George Bell, the figure at the centre of this storm is of enormous significance in the history of the Church's vocation to speak out prophetically as well as pastorally in moments of crisis and opportunity. Bell did both. His association with Dietrich Bonhoeffer, his courageous opposition to area bombing during the Second World War, his support for resistance to fascism, his assistance to displaced persons and refugees who had fled the continent, and his vision of post-war reconciliation in Europe are among his chief claims to fame.

Bell also advocated for both German and British conscientious objectors and was a significant pioneer of the ecumenical movement. His theological work in these and other contexts remains valuable. In short, George Kennedy Allen Bell (4 February 1883 – 3 October 1958) Dean of Canterbury, Bishop of Chichester, member of the House of Lords, is someone who, while a man of his time and generation, can and should speak to us in another quite different time of challenge and brooding darkness.

However, this important legacy was almost overcome and overshadowed by what the subtitle of this important book rightly calls 'the Church's flawed case against Bishop George Bell'. *Presumption of Guilt* has been carefully compiled and written by someone with personal and family knowledge of those impacted by it. As Ruth Grayson says, "Bell's reputation was unfairly and unjustifiably traduced by people who were, and in some cases still are, in positions of both influence and authority both within the Church and in wider society." It is important that the story of how this happened, and what has been needed for restitution and recovery, is told.

The other dimension of all this is the vexed issue of the Church and its implication in historical abuse and serious safeguarding flaws. In July 2019, Ekklesia Publishing produced the book *Letters to a Broken Church,* edited by Janet Fife and 'Gilo'. This was a harrowing set of accounts from abuse survivors and their allies of failings within the Church of England, in particular. The recent long-overdue publication of the Makin Report and the circumstances surrounding the widespread abuse committed by John Smyth QC has only emphasised its significance and verdict. Yet it was survivors themselves who felt that a chapter in their book should also address the Bell saga, and the link between the failure to address serious abuse within the Church and its attempt to rush through a flawed case against a public figure from the past in what many saw as an act of deflection.

As the publisher, I would like to express heartfelt thanks to Ruth Grayson, Keith Clements and all the others mentioned in these pages who have worked so hard to ensure that justice and right should prevail in the Bell case, and that the Church should face the continuing challenge of truth-telling and justice-making for all whose lives and reputations have been damaged amidst the failure to address such matters properly. May Bishop George Bell's witness live on, and may this book be another small step in achieving change within both our understanding and our institutional life.

Simon Barrow
Ekklesia Publishing

ACKNOWLEDGEMENTS

Many people have been involved, in many different ways, in the course of the campaign which began in October 2015 to obtain justice for the late Bishop George Bell and to clear his name afterward. Some, but not all, of those with whom I myself worked or came into contact are mentioned in these pages. There are others who have written to the press, signed petitions and attended meetings and demonstrations whose names do not appear here. Regretfully, it is not possible to name everyone.

But two people in particular must be mentioned, who – although they were not involved in the production of the present book – deserve particular recognition and thanks for the part they played in obtaining justice for George Bell. They were less involved than some others in the more public aspects of the campaign. But their painstaking and meticulous behind-the-scenes work had a decisive influence on its outcome. These are Professor Andrew Chandler and Desmond Browne KC, whose detailed professional knowledge of Bell's life on the one hand and of the law on the other were undoubtedly fundamental in persuading the church authorities concerned to commission the independent review of the processes involved undertaken by Lord Carlile, and who played a key role in challenging the subsequent proceedings as well. I regret that I have written little about them, perhaps because their many endeavours were mostly kept out of the public domain. I am grateful to both of them for reading and responding positively to the earlier unpublished version of this book *Balance Of Improbabilities: A Personal Perspective On The George Bell Case*.

Otherwise, I am confining these acknowledgements specifically to those who helped bring this work to fruition. The Rev Dr Barry Orford kindly commented on the first draft of the initial unpublished volume. Kat Taylor proofread that version, the cover of which was designed by Leon Russell. The photograph on page xiii has been reproduced by kind permission of Bildagentur in Berlin. The original photograph also shows The Rev Eric Loveday, the vicar of St Martin-in-the-Fields, where George Bell and Franz Hildebrandt were participating in the commemorative service as described in the caption.

The Rev Dr Keith Clements has brought his own expertise to bear in writing the chapter in the present book introducing Bell and chronicling the case against him, which was missing from my first effort. I am grateful to my publisher, Simon Barrow at Ekklesia Publishing, for this suggestion. I am also grateful to Lord Carlile, who corrected me (gently) on my definition of the difference between civil and criminal law in that earlier version. I fear he may still find fault with it… although as I have noted in self-defence, I am not a lawyer!

Above all, I am indebted to friends in the Chichester area who supported this endeavour and whose hospitality during my visits to the city made it possible to complete it. Most especially I would like to record my heartfelt thanks to three people who sadly are no longer with us: Marilyn and Peter Billingham, and Clare Toole-Mackson. Finally, I must pay tribute to my long-suffering husband, James, not only for his own part in the public face of the campaign but in putting up with endless conversations on the subject within the confines of our own home. For the better part of a decade, this issue has dominated our lives. I hope that, with the publication of this book, we may be helping to ensure that the gross miscarriage of justice that took place in the George Bell affair will never happen again.

Ruth Hildebrandt Grayson

ACKNOWLEDGEMENTS

George Bell and Franz Hildebrandt at St Martin-in-the-Fields, London, in July 1941, on the occasion of a service marking the third anniversary of the imprisonment of Martin Niemöller in Sachsenhausen concentration camp (reproduced by kind permission of Bildagentur, Berlin).

PREFACE

This little book is an updated and extended version of my earlier unpublished effort *Balance Of Improbabilities: A Personal Perspective On The George Bell Case,* first privately circulated in 2023. It includes a new addition: a chapter introducing Bishop George Bell written by The Rev Dr Keith Clements, to whom I am deeply indebted. My previous venture had been written on the premise that my selected readers – specifically family members and personal friends as well as some of those with whom I had come into contact in the course of the struggle to obtain justice for George Bell and then to clear his name of the unsubstantiated posthumous charge against him – would know who he was. I hope the present book will be of interest to a wider readership too. Keith Clements's contribution expertly fills one gap in my original text.

I had been hesitant about seeking formal publication of the book. It had not been my original intention to do so. The case is over, some restitution has begun to take place, and some of the widespread anger generated by the affair has dissipated. So why do it?

There are several reasons. The first one is possibly the most important. Mud sticks. Bell's reputation was unfairly and unjustifiably traduced by people who were, and in some cases still are, in positions of both influence and authority both within the Church and in wider society. There have been as yet no unreserved apologies from most of those responsible for this. The restitution that has taken place to date, most notably the restoration of George Bell's name to the building from which it was peremptorily removed in 2015, has largely been brought about by individuals who had not themselves been responsible for its removal. More is still needed. Bell's name may still be associated with child sexual abuse both now and in the future, for example by schoolchildren whose house was suddenly renamed after October 2015, and by many of the visitors to the cathedral who bought the misleading 2016 edition of the guide. An open and unambiguous apology from those individuals who did most to traduce the late bishop's reputation is needed to correct this misinformation once and for all. So far this has not been forthcoming.

Until it is, and even if it is, there is an obvious need for more published material about the case itself to be in the public domain, written by those with much greater expertise than mine to do so and with access to the records of the diocesan proceedings and the relevant documents, which I do not currently have. As well as setting the record straight in this instance, such works may help to ensure that greater care will be taken by church authorities in future cases to follow correct procedures and thus to allow justice to take its proper course. My own concern with the affair arose from my father's personal friendship with the late bishop. Since I had no specialist expertise to bring to the affair, the primary focus of the present book is the publicity surrounding the case rather than the case itself. It is solely based on some of the correspondence it generated in the press and in unpublished letters exchanged with certain key players, together with some personal observations. I hope that its publication may prompt others to write their own accounts on the basis of their far more expert knowledge and legally relevant documents.

False accusations do a lot of harm, not just to the reputation of the accused – and in those cases where the individual is alive, to their careers and indeed their whole lives as well – but also to their families, friends and supporters. The church officials involved in this instance, as in other instances of safeguarding, needed to reflect that it was not just the complainant to whom they had a duty of pastoral care. The fact that members of Bell's family only heard about the case through the press once the diocese of Chichester had reached its unwarranted conclusion is disgraceful. Bell's most recent biographer Prof Andrew Chandler (who lives close at hand in the Chichester area) and the late bishop's former chaplain at the relevant time were likewise never consulted. In particular, the chaplain, Canon Adrian Carey, who was still alive and entirely *compos mentis* when news of the case broke, had known Bell both professionally and personally and had worked closely with him during most of the time in question. His evidence would almost certainly have been conclusive had it ever been sought. Such omissions alone are striking indicators of the degree of mismanagement with which the case was handled.

Since 2015, more cases have come to light both within the Church of England and other denominations in which there have been clear miscarriages of justice. These have affected not only living defendants but their families and friends, whose lives have all been disrupted if not completely ruined. A number of defendants have given up church work, despite there being no case against them. Divorces have occurred and families have been broken up. There has been at least one instance of the suicide of an ordained priest following an unsubstantiated allegation of abuse against him.

So this case has relevance in the wider sphere as well. Safeguarding in the Church of England, as in other denominations, is under constant scrutiny because its record has been so poor in the past. Yet the various attempts to reform it, to implement the recommendations of the IICSA report and particularly to establish an independent oversight system, have so far come to nothing. It is almost as if the Church is afraid to take the necessary action, perhaps for fear of the possibility that more cases will come to light and will inflict even more damage on its reputation. Instead, it seems to place an undue emphasis on perhaps more peripheral matters as (for instance) the often unnecessary and overly intrusive scrutiny of church staff and volunteers, followed up by copious training materials and courses. A whole safeguarding industry has taken root with the creation of new departments, new jobs, new roles and a vast over-commitment of dwindling resources both nationally and locally. On many church websites, safeguarding features more prominently than details about pastoral assistance and service information. Ironically, much of this was put in place by the former Archbishop of Canterbury, who found himself having to resign over his failure to pass on his knowledge of the abuse perpetrated by the late John Smyth.

And yet abuse continues, in the Church as elsewhere. The fact is that whatever measures may be put in place, an abuser is adept at operating below the radar, and may only surface when the victim eventually has the courage to speak out. The safeguarding procedures so far in place in the Church often seem to be aimed at the wrong people, numbers of whom are put off volunteering their services as a result. Meanwhile, Church officials – sometimes at the highest level – have been found to be guilty of double standards, not passing information to the appropriate authorities at the appropriate time and in some cases covering up for individuals while knowing of their abuse. The Makin report on the John Smyth affair, just published on 7 November 2024), illustrates this point. (Keith Makin, *Independent Learning Lessons Review: John Smyth QC, 18 October 2024* [online])

Moreover, miscarriages of justice – whether in safeguarding or in other areas – are not confined to churches or other religious bodies. This book is being published not only against the background of the fallout from the Makin report but also against the background of the ongoing Horizon IT scandal in the Post Office, which was brought most urgently to public attention in January 2024 in the ITV series featuring the heroic efforts of former sub-postmaster Sir Alan Bates and the investigative journalism of Gwyneth Hughes. Safeguarding may not be the issue here, but false accusations and resultant miscarriages of justice certainly are. The Post Office, like the Church, is an institution from which we might have expected better. Instead, there remains a failure to apologise on the part of some of the key players (largely on grounds of pleading ignorance to what was going on) as well as a failure to hasten the payment of compensation to the hundreds of victims involved.

Like the Church in the George Bell affair, the Post Office seems to have responded in accordance with its own law and to have acted as both judge and jury toward so many of its innocent employees. Like the Church, it has ruined lives. Maybe, like the Church, it has its own reasons for dragging its feet in bringing about restitution to its victims. Chief among these in both cases may well be fear of losing face. Yet in the Church at any rate, a willingness to confess wrongdoing and to repent of it is basic to Christian teaching. This might possibly do more than even the most ardent evangelistic programme to reverse its continuing numerical decline. The saying 'practise what you preach' springs to mind here.

Meanwhile, in the Bell case, the passage of time itself increases the very real possibility not only that the whole affair but that the man himself may all but be forgotten. Already there are many people, ordained clergy included, who have never heard of him; or if they have, it is as likely to be for the wrong reasons as for the right ones at the present time. I shared with a number of my fellow campaigners a perhaps cynical feeling that one reason for the slow progress toward restitution was that many of those who knew and cared most about the restoration of Bell's reputation tended to be in their later years, and were likely not to be around too much longer. Thus the whole matter could be kicked into the long grass and eventually buried. Sadly, several of our number have indeed now died. It is out of a sense of loyalty to them that I have felt impelled all the more urgently to see this project through to publication.

Ruth Hildebrandt Grayson
February 2025

INTRODUCTION
A Prophet With Honour: Who Was George Bell and Why Does He Matter?

Keith Clements

'George Kennedy Allen Bell – Bishop of Chichester 1929–1958 – A True Pastor – Poet and Patron of the Arts – Champion of the Oppressed and Tireless Worker for Christian Unity.'

EACH PHRASE ON George Bell's epitaph in Chichester Cathedral reflects a vital aspect of his unusual career. A life of restless, exhausting activity? In fact he also exhibited a special quality, vividly captured in a pen portrait by the Swedish archbishop Nathan Söderblom at an international conference in Oud Wassenaar, Holland, in 1919:

> [Bell] sat just opposite me. He said hardly anything except when he was asked. Then, after consideration, he gave a thoughtful answer which always proved to be reliable. The face is dominated by two large, round eyes, which shine with the life and soul behind and indicate a rich inner life. In my opinion, no man means more for the ecumenical awakening than this silent Bell. This Bell never rings unnecessarily. But when it sounds, the tone is silvery clear. It is heard. It penetrates more than many boisterous voices. He does not speak without having something to say. The strong spirituality of his personality marks everything that he does.

That conference, called by the World Alliance for International Friendship Through the Churches to promote reconciliation after the 1914–18 war, marked George Bell's entry, at age 36, onto the international ecumenical stage.

Background and History

He was born in 1883, his father an Anglican clergyman. Right from his student days at Oxford he displayed a passion for poetry, social issues and Christian unity, and was ordained priest in 1907. Soon after the outbreak of war in August 1914 he was appointed chaplain to the archbishop of Canterbury, Randall Davidson. The archbishop was increasingly sympathetic to ecumenical aspirations and concern for the wider world, and Bell became his right-hand assistant in pursuit of these. The war inflicted an especially personal grief on Bell, with the loss of his brothers Donald and Benedict, killed in France in April 1918. That year also brought him the lasting happiness of marriage to Henrietta ('Hettie') Livingstone. Following the Armistice, he was soon immersed in the churches' international efforts for reconciliation and social justice, and was the archbishop's appointed delegate at the Oud Wassenaar conference.

In 1924 he was appointed dean of Canterbury Cathedral, a post which increased his personal stature and enabled him to pursue the ecumenical projects close to his heart and to found the Canterbury Festival of Music and Drama. In 1925 the 'Life and Work' Conference for justice and international peace met at Stockholm under the leadership of Nathan Söderblom. Before the conference closed it was Bell who made the decisive intervention urging the formation of a more permanent body to study and implement its aims. This eventuated in the formation of the Universal Christian Council for Life and Work. Bell was elected to its executive committee and set about implementing the vision of Life and Work at home, getting the Church of England to create its own Council on Foreign Relations, and initiating a series of conferences between British and German theologians. In 1928 he was consecrated and appointed bishop of Chichester.

In 1932 Bell was elected chairman of the Council of Life and Work. He was now at the helm of the largest and most inclusively representative international ecumenical body yet in being, and was thus the personalised voice of the growing movement for unity and service to the world. It was a critical moment. New crises were about to break on the world, particularly in Europe, which would radically challenge the young ecumenical fellowship. The executive committee of Life and Work met in Berlin in late January 1933, the very moment when Adolf Hitler came to power as chancellor of Germany. Bell saw at first hand the nationalist excitement that spilled onto the streets, and was not impressed by the positive gloss put on it by some German colleagues. During the following months the violent manifestations of antisemitism, the rise of the so-called 'German Christian' movement with its demands for 'Aryanisation' of the church (i.e. expelling people of Jewish descent from office), and all the signs of an emerging police state, were more than enough to alarm Christian opinion outside Germany; not to mention Hitler's appointment of Ludwig Müller, a theologically illiterate former naval chaplain and staunch Nazi, as 'Reich bishop'.

Bell and the majority on the Life and Work executive perceived the scenario not only as a threat to German Protestantism but of deep concern to Christians everywhere. In the face of fierce opposition from such as Theodor Heckel, head of the Reich Church's foreign relations department, Bell diplomatically but firmly maintained that the 'Church Struggle' was a legitimate concern to churches outside Germany. At the Life and Work executive meeting in September Bell as chairman moved a resolution recording the great anxieties of churches in Europe and North America 'in particular with regard to the severe action taken against persons of Jewish origin' and the 'serious restrictions placed upon freedom of thought and expression in Germany'. This was passed but with Heckel recording his dissent.

Bell and Bonhoeffer

In October Bell's efforts to give ecumenical support to those who inside Germany were resisting the Nazi pressure on the churches were greatly strengthened by the arrival in London of the young theologian Dietrich Bonhoeffer as pastor of two German congregations. His stay there lasted two years. Bell found in Bonhoeffer a channel of first-hand, almost daily, information on the German scene. In turn Bonhoeffer found in Bell the ecumenical leader who like no other could publicly and on the international stage voice the plight of those Germans under increasing pressures of harassment and imprisonment. This was the start of a deep and lasting personal friendship. Bonhoeffer was joined in London for a time by another young pastor, Franz Hildebrandt, a close friend from their student days together in Berlin.

Hildebrandt was later to return to the UK as a refugee in 1937, not only on account of his own key role in the German church resistance movement but also on account of his 'non-Aryan' lineage. Bell affectionately referred to them as 'my two boys' (the Bells themselves were childless). Part of the impetus behind the present book was the wish of Hildebrandt's daughter Ruth Grayson to commemorate that friendship.

In response to urgent pleas from the threatened pastors in Germany, and from Bonhoeffer, on Ascension Day, 10 May 1934, Bell as President Bell of Life and Work issued a pastoral letter to all its member churches calling attention to the measures being taken 'against Ministers of the Gospel on account of their loyalty to the fundamental principles of Christian truth', and the need for prayerful solidarity with them. Bell had consulted in depth with Bonhoeffer on the precise wording. It was the first public ecumenical comment on the Church Struggle, being published in sections of the secular press and warmly welcomed in Germany by those suffering for their stand. Three weeks later the German Evangelical (i.e. Protestant) Confessing Synod met at Barmen, issuing the famous Barmen Theological Declaration opposing the Nazification of the Church and signalling the formation of the Confessing Church.

In August the full Life and Work Council met on the Danish Island of Fanö. High on the agenda was the preparation for the next world conference of Life and Work, on 'Church, Community and State' to take place in Oxford in 1937 under the skilled guidance of the lay ecumenical pioneer J.H. Oldham. The topic was obviously of increasing relevance given the trends towards state autocracy across the world, and most urgent was the current German Church scene. Under Bell's clear-sighted chairing, and in the face (again) of the hostility of Theodor Heckel and a representative of the 'German Christians', intensive debate resulted in an endorsement of Bell's Ascension Day message, and a resolution of solidarity with the witness of the Confessing Church. Fanö, remarks historian Andrew Chandler, perhaps marked 'Bell's greatest achievement in ecumenical statecraft'. Ecumenism here had been steered irrevocably away from a safe, subservient neutrality towards a committed embrace of the truth under oppression. Bell continued to further the cause of the Confessing Church at meetings of the Life and Work executive and the 1937 Oxford Conference.

In 1938 Bell, in due order of seniority of bishops, took his seat in the House of Lords. He now had a recognised platform on the national as well as ecclesiastical stage and immediately put this into effect with a speech on refugees. While President of Life and Work in 1933, he had become chair of the International Christian Commission for Refugees. By the outbreak of war in 1939 an estimated 80,000 refugees from Nazi Germany and Czechoslovakia were in Britain, mainly Jews but also intellectual and political opponents of the Nazi regime. From the outset Bell had a passionate but often frustrated concern for all such, campaigning persistently but with limited success in getting the Church of England and other British churches to raise enough funds for their support, and for government to act more humanely and generously in their reception and support. It was not a popular cause in Britain.

In February 1939 he was invited to address the Jewish Historical Society and chose the topic 'Humanity and the Refugees'. Of specific concern to him were the 'non-Aryan' Christians, both pastors and laypeople, who had been in no less danger than those categorised simply as Jews but whose status and needs were not always recognised by the reception organisations in Britain. Bell effectively became their sponsor and guardian, in many cases at an exhaustingly personal as well as organizational level. After the outbreak of war the plight of the German refugees was compounded by their indiscriminate treatment as 'enemy aliens', many of them suffering internment regardless of their being victims – or indeed stated opponents – of the regime. Bell visited their internment camp on the Isle of Man to see conditions for himself, and spoke vigorously on the injustice of the policy. This earned him unpopularity in sections of the press where he was dubbed 'the self-appointed champion of captive Nazis and Fascists'.

During the two years preceding the outbreak of war in September 1939 Bell like many other church and political leaders in Britain supported the policy of 'appeasement' not out of any sympathy with Nazism but in the hope that the catastrophe of 1914–18 might not be repeated. As late as May 1940 he was still hoping in the possibility of a negotiated peace, but Hitler's westward invasions put paid to that. From then on, he had no doubt that the military defeat of Hitler was necessary for peace in Europe.

That same year, when the starkest peril of the war burst upon Britain, his paperback *Christianity and World Order* was published. Drawing much on the 1937 Oxford Conference, it distils his wide-ranging thinking on Christian faith; on the church and the ecumenical movement in response to the unprecedented challenges of the war; peace aims; the church and the future; and the personal Christian life of responsibility in the world: 'A great search is proceeding side by side with the War. It is a search for world order, and for such a world order as shall satisfy the real needs, alike of the individual and of the community. . . What is wanted now is an unflinching belief in God, and an unlimited love of my neighbour. They must go together.' Within three years the book had sold 80,000 copies. Some found their way to neutral countries and to the World Council of Churches (WCC) in Geneva, where Dietrich Bonhoeffer read it gratefully while visiting there in 1941.

The German Resistance

In May 1942 Bell made an extended visit to neutral Sweden under the auspices of the British government's Ministry of Information which was seeking to foster links between different departments of British and Swedish cultural life. He met with a number of Swedish ecumenists. But one day, in the lakeside town of Sigtuna, to his astonishment Dietrich Bonhoeffer appeared. Now actively involved as an international courier for the German political conspiracy to overthrow Hitler, Bonhoeffer had been on his third wartime visit to the WCC in Geneva, and while there heard that Bell was in Sweden. Rushing back to Berlin he discussed with leading political and military members of the conspiracy the possibilities that might be offered for the resistance by a meeting with Bell. Travel permits were obtained, and soon Bonhoeffer landed in Sweden. Bell had been hearing from others in Sweden about the German resistance, but what Bonhoeffer now told him amplified and confirmed its significance as only someone like Bonhoeffer could. This was with a view to Bell passing on the information to the British government, in the hope that the Allies might signal that in the event of a successful overthrow of the regime they would negotiate a peace with a non-Nazi government. Bonhoeffer also shared with Bell his personal situation. Bell's fears for him now deepened immeasurably.

Back in London, in a personal meeting Bell relayed to the Foreign

Secretary Anthony Eden what he had learnt from Bonhoeffer. There was some sympathy, but the Foreign Office was not persuaded. Were these approaches any more than indirect peace-feelers from the regime? It had been agreed in Sigtuna that Bell would communicate the London response in a coded message to Geneva. Sadly, it was negative. This did not mean a complete stop to Bell's efforts. In public he persistently argued the case for there being 'another Germany' than the Nazi version. Could not the government at least give some recognition and encouragement to those Germans working for an overthrow and a just peace? But the Allied line was that only Germany's unconditional surrender and total disarmament could guarantee a non-Nazi Germany. Nevertheless Bell did not give up, and on 10 March 1943 he made a powerful speech in the House of Lords, challenging the government on whether it made a distinction 'between the Hitler state and the German people in their prosecution of the war and their view of our war aims?' Dissent in Germany, he declared, had not been totally terrorised into submission, and hope should be given to those Germans secretly striving against the regime.

The Area Bombing

The wartime issue perhaps most famously associated with Bell was the area bombing of German cities. Right at the start of the war, in his *Diocesan Gazette* he had welcomed the stated commitment of the British and French governments that any aerial bombardments would be strictly limited to military objectives. He warned: 'It is barbarous to make unarmed women and children the deliberate object of attack . . . If Europe is civilised at all, what can excuse the bombing of towns by night and the terrorising of non-combatants who work by day and cannot sleep when darkness comes?' But by 1943 the British night-bombing offensive was being pursued relentlessly, especially in the spring against the industrial towns of the Ruhr, followed by Hamburg in July, and in December Berlin itself. Overall, vast stretches were laid waste, and an estimated 410,00 civilians were killed by the offensive – 49,000 in Hamburg alone, and 35,000 in Berlin. British public opinion generally acquiesced in the policy, not just because London and other cities had suffered from German bombing but because, according to the official line, the only way to win the war was to destroy the industrial base of the

German war effort, and the only way to do that was by bombing.

It was Bell's House of Lords speech on 9 February 1944 which caused the greatest public stir. Bell was not a pacifist, and he prefaced his speech by paying tribute to the personal courage and skill of the air crews involved (upwards of 20,000 British airmen died in the offensive). His opposition to the policy was based on a careful application of the traditional Christian Just War Doctrine, including the stipulation that the means employed in war must be proportionate to the goal, and above all the requirement to discriminate between combatants and non-combatants: a distinction, he asserted, that the British government had repeatedly claimed to recognise. So Bell questioned the morality of obliterating whole towns simply because certain parts of it contained military or strategic industrial targets, a policy that itself smacked of the Nazi philosophy that Might was Right, and contrary to the British government's own declared commitments: 'The Allies', he declared, 'stand for something greater than power. The chief name inscribed on our banner is "Law".'

A few other bishops agreed with his views but did not publicly address the matter in like manner. Archbishop William Temple was a confirmed supporter of the bombing. Strident accusations of undermining the war effort were vented on Bell in the press and in correspondence arriving at Chichester. It was a pinnacle moment of speaking truth to power. When eight months later the see of Canterbury fell vacant with the unexpected death of William Temple, many felt that Bell was the obvious candidate to succeed him. But it was Geoffrey Fisher, bishop of London, who was translated to Canterbury. There have been rumours ever since that prime minister Churchill would not countenance such a troublesome prelate as Bell, and that it was his stand against the bombing policy that had cost him his preferment.

The Post-War Future of Europe and the Churches

In May 1945 the end of war in Europe brought both relief and sadness. There came the news that Dietrich Bonhoeffer and his brother Klaus had been executed. At their memorial service on July 27 in London, broadcast by the BBC to Germany, George Bell preached in English, followed by Franz Hildebrandt in German. Three months later George Bell was the senior figure in the delegation of ecumenical representatives who met in Stuttgart with leaders of the German Evangelical Church. The Germans present, all of whom had served in the Confessing Church, in some cases to the point of imprisonment, included Martin Niemöller who had endured eight years in concentration camp. On both sides there were understandable misgivings, but Bell from the start breathed friendship. The memory of Bonhoeffer, with his repeated emphasis on the church's calling to confess its own guilt, was an effectual presence. The Germans volunteered a poignant statement confessing their own failure to witness more courageously against National Socialism: 'Now a new beginning is to be made in our churches'. Abroad their statement was held up as further evidence that there was indeed 'another Germany' to that of the swastika. It was a notable step in post-war reconciliation.

Continuing in Prophetic Ecumenical Mode

Other issues kept Bell in prophetic mode. His role as a bishop, he said, was not that of 'saying ditto to the state'. He had publicly protested against the dropping of the atomic bombs on Japan, and was a member of the British Council of Churches group, led by J.H. Oldham, which produced the report *The Era of Atomic Power,* speaking at its launch in 1946. Central to his concerns were reconstruction in Europe and the consolidation of the World Council of Churches still 'in formation'. In August 1948, ten years after its constitution had been laid down came the full inauguration of the WCC at its first assembly in Amsterdam. While relatively inconspicuous in the immediate preparations and at the Assembly itself, Bell was truly one of its enablers. Visser't Hooft, first general secretary of the WCC, said that without Bell – and Stuttgart – there would have been no Amsterdam. He was appointed first moderator of the central committee. On the public stage in Britain, his dissenting role continued in his severe criticism of British policy over Cyprus and his support of Archbishop Makarios who was leading the Greek Cypriot cause for independence. Bell had to face accusations in Parliament that he was more loyal to the WCC than to British interests. No less was he critical of British policy during the Suez Crisis of 1956.

Loyal to the World Council of Churches he certainly was, and the WCC at its second Assembly in 1954 underlined its gratitude by electing him one of its Presidents. As such he died in 1958 in Canterbury, having just retired there from Chichester.

'I Seek My Brethren': Further Reflections

George Bell is commemorated in prayer on 3 October each year throughout the worldwide Anglican communion. A great, even the greatest, Anglican bishop of the twentieth century as many would say? That he should be so highly estimated would have no doubt surprised him. He was well aware of the controversies he had aroused, both within the church and in society, and what he felt to be the limited nature of his achievements. But if the role of a bishop is to lead as a shepherd leads his flock, he exemplified like few others have done the courage and vision required to lead the flock not just through the familiar green pastures but onto the rocky hillsides, caught by a wider vision and seeking a deeper faithfulness to the call of Christ in the modern world. Writing of Bell's rootedness in his Anglican tradition, Andrew Chandler says: 'Bell gave a new, urgent form to what he inherited and found about him: he developed, enriched, and applied and, in so doing, made what he inherited into something greater than it had been, something that could be received by men and women at large in the world, and something that possessed the power to endure'. Crucial to that vision was his ecumenism. For him, the bedrock ecclesial loyalty was to the one universal church of Christ, within which his being an Anglican was held and nurtured. 'I seek my brethren', the text (Genesis 37:16) on which he chose to preach at his installation as Dean of Canterbury Cathedral on 21 March 1924, signalled his life's theme.

Most strikingly it led him into utmost solidarity with the German Confessing Church and its challenge to the ecumenical movement at world level. His clandestine meeting with Dietrich Bonhoeffer in Sweden in 1942 was not *only* a matter of receiving information about the conspiracy to overthrow Hitler (hugely important indeed) but an occasion for something much deeper, as Bonhoeffer bared the anguish of his soul at his country's guilt, Christians no less than others, and their need to bear the judgment of God should that fall upon them in the chaos of defeat: 'Oh, we must be punished'. This was in effect a confessional ministered by Bell the confessor, pastor and priest. 'Very moving was our talk, very moving our last farewell. And the last letter I had from him, just before he returned to

INTRODUCTION A Prophet With Honour: Who Was George Bell and Why Does He Matter?

Berlin, knowing what might await him there, I will treasure for the whole of my life'. That memory certainly inspired Bell at the 1945 Stuttgart meeting. Bell was effectively remodelling ecumenism as not confined to formal statements and agreements (important) or even to cooperative action (very important) but expressed in relationships, personal and communal, at the deepest level; of bearing one another's burdens of pain, guilt and the need for mutual forgiveness as the way of hope.

'Unshakeable friend' is the apt description of Bell in that context, used by Edwin Robertson as the title of his book on Bell and the German churches. The quality of that friendship was apparent at much wider levels too. Twice Bell, who had welcomed Gandhi to Chichester, visited India. He vigorously supported the formation of the Church of South India (in face of Anglo-Catholic opposition) and central to his interests were his Indian friends themselves. After Bell's death Russell Chandran, sometime principal of the United Theological College at Bangalore, wrote to Henrietta Bell: 'Bishop Bell always impressed me as a "humble man of God"... The way he made inquiries about his friends in India showed the amount of personal affection he held for people. He always made me feel that he was a personal friend, not just a great man.'

Much has obviously had to be left out of this short account of Bell. It is to be hoped that what emerges is how as a pastoral yet prophetic leader Bell was able to see the essentials of an issue and to hold together seemingly divergent elements in the Christian response. He was no sentimentalist. For him the call to love had to be in harness with justice: 'Justice and Order are in effect the necessary groundwork on which Love is to build. Those who undermine or violate Justice and Order are making the rule of Love immensely, if not impossibly, difficult to secure or continue.' He was great in his ability to hold together both these essentials of Christian witness. And for him the Christian struggle was for the safeguarding not of religion, but of humanity: 'The Church has still a special duty to be a watchman for humanity, and to plead the cause of the suffering, whether Jew or Gentile'. That motivated particularly his work for refugees, for which private charity alone was inadequate and required political and economic ordering – 'For the problem of the refugee is the problem of humanity'. His identification of the church's mission as the 'watchman for humanity' points to the need, even when Christians are most fervent in their religiously-empowered zeal, for seeking a platform with others on which to build alliances for the common good of humanity.

In 1943 he presided over a meeting of the World Congress of Faiths, and both there and in the House of Lords called on representatives of the great world religions to come together after the war and take counsel in joint endeavours for peace. Equally telling is what he says in his sermon at the memorial service for Dietrich Bonhoeffer, for it displays his own like aspiration and his rejection of any notion that Christians have a monopoly on humanitarian and liberal ideals: 'As one of a noble company of martyrs of differing traditions, [Bonhoeffer] represents both the resistance of the believing soul, in the name of God, to the assault of evil, and also the moral and political revolt of the human conscience against injustice and cruelty.'

Bell for his part did not argue for a radically new understanding of the relation of the church, including its established form, to the state. He was simply assuming and exemplifying where the church's primary loyalty lay, as the Body of Christ in the world. Whether on refugees, or the bombing of civilians, or the British post-war policy on Cyprus he was exercising the sovereign freedom of a Christian priest and bishop to speak truth to power, without regard to the consequences for himself. As such he is inspirational for today and tomorrow.

Why Keep His Memory Alive Now?

Some of the issues that exercised Bell issues are too obviously with us still: refugees and asylum seekers to be treated justly and humanely; autocracies and dictatorships to be resisted; religious nationalism repeating the mistakes made in 1930s Germany. As this is being written, innocent civilians are again suffering intense bombing in Ukraine and the Middle East. Bell, who embodied dissent according to conscience, still speaks. The complacent assumption that things as they are in society are best left alone, together with the notion that faith is a purely private affair of the individual and has no role in the public sphere (other than to respect the status quo) remains endemic. This habitually slides into the belief that *institutions* are exempt from moral scrutiny in their corporate behaviour and policies. Bell is as relevant as ever in pointing the need for agencies in every area of life to be morally accountable at the bar of humanity. (The Post Office rushing to judgment on the alleged embezzlement by its sub-postmasters and -mistresses, and its long resistance to acknowledging its responsibility, is a case in point).

There are no no-go areas for ethics. A watchperson for humanity is always needed. A church which does not respond to that call has lost its soul, and a society which does not heed it will lose itself. What is needed here is not just a compilation of the list of issues on which Bell can be considered 'relevant'. It is also a matter of cherishing the inner quality of that mind and heart and spirit which so impressed Nathan Söderblom at Oud Wassenaar in 1919, and so many others thereafter; the calm face which saw and heard so much and the voice which uttered only what was essential and to the point, come what may.

Yet, more than six decades after his death, can a figure like Bell, however admired, really be partner and mentor in our current engagements? It is not just the passage of time separating us from him. We are now, many argue, in the *post-colonial* age; whereas Bell was born into British society and culture when the empire was at its height, and still powerful when he died. 'Colonialism' is now seen in critical view as an ideology and culture which lives on subtly but strongly long after the British empire. It assumes a western dominance in thought and in understanding of history, with a disregard for the diversity of traditions and perspectives found elsewhere especially in the global south. Western Christianity, on this view, itself needs to be decolonised in its theology and practice. Bell being a person of his age, moreover a bishop of the English established church of that time, may be assumed to be a product and promoter of the 'colonial' mentality that desires to impose uniformity, suppressing diversity and unaware of what is truly 'other' in one's neighbours. What should be done is to look carefully at Bell's actual record, in order to discern points at which he does not quite fit the overall 'colonial' narrative and the top-down establishment model; at why he has been called 'the paradigm of creative dissent'.

As for diversity, let us end where we began, with his memorial plaque in Chichester Cathedral, which places his patronage of the arts (which by their very nature manifest diversity) even before his work for the oppressed and for Christian unity. Himself a poet, he was determined to bring into view the artists, poets, dramatists and musicians whose genius springs out of creative freedom, regardless of their religious outlook if any, and whom he saw as vital to human flourishing. Memorably he described the arts as 'auxiliaries of the Gospel', to be encouraged in making their own contribution in disclosing and celebrating the human condition. This is but one among many reasons for caution against dismissing Bell from the post-colonial age which, like any other, is in need of human enrichment.

Why it is Important to Set the Record Straight

The need to uphold George Bell's stature suddenly and unexpectedly became urgent on 23 October 2015, when headlines appeared in the English press such as 'Eminent bishop was paedophile, admits Church'. The Church of England Media Centre had released a statement that the present bishop of Chichester, Dr Martin Warner, had a made a public apology to someone who alleged they had been sexually abused over a period of time in the 1940s and 1950s by George Bell. The church authorities proceeded quickly to remove Bell's name and image from church-related buildings and the Chichester city council chamber. The story of how Bell's name so quickly and irresponsibly became tarnished, and of how eventually, after eight years of campaigning by supporters of Bell from different walks of life and church tradition, was restored, is told by Ruth Grayson in the following pages. Suffice it to say that the allegation was revealed to have been a rush to judgment on the part of the church authorities, without any substantial evidence, and was pursued in a woefully incompetent and superficial way.

Members of the George Bell Group, which had been formed to press for a proper investigation, were criticised by some of the church authorities for seemingly wanting to privilege Bell and protest his innocence on the grounds of his fame. This was not so. They simply wished the investigation to be reviewed properly by a qualified lawyer acceptable to the Church (Lord Alex Carlile QC was duly appointed). But what was seriously hurtful was the incongruity that Bell, who in his life had such an outstanding record of seeking justice on behalf of the oppressed, should in death be subject himself to a gross miscarriage of reputational justice. It was not just the standing of Bell, but the moral standing of the church, that was at stake, A church so careless of the memory of its greatest leaders and teachers jeopardises its own moral standing, betraying scant regard for justice at large. That is why it matters to remember and uphold the late Bishop George Bell.

For Further Reading

Andrew Chandler, *George Bell, Bishop of Chichester. Church, State and Resistance in the Age of Dictatorship* (Wm B. Eerdmans, 2016).

Keith Clements, J.H. Oldham and George Bell, *Ecumenical Pioneers* (Fortress Press 2022).

Edwin Robertson, *Unshakeable Friend. George Bell and the German Churches* (CTBI, 1995).

Ronald C.D. Jasper, *George Bell, Bishop of Chichester* (OUP, 1967).

CHAPTER ONE
In the Beginning…

WE THOUGHT IT must have been a misprint.

On 22 October 2015, a statement was released, completely out of the blue, by the Church of England. It said that the late Bishop George Bell of Chichester had been declared guilty 'on the balance of probabilities' of the alleged sexual abuse on numerous occasions between 1948 and 1951 of a single complainant, who was a young child at the time of the imputed misconduct. There had been no previous publicity, and no hint of what was to come.

Nobody had known anything about the allegation outside the claimant's own circle, those to whom she had taken the complaint, and those whom the Church had charged with handling it on her behalf. The late bishop's own family had not been informed. Mrs Barbara Whitley, Bell's niece, wrote to me in 2018 that *'The first I knew about "Carol" [the complainant] was when Charles Moore wrote in The Times in October 2015 about her being paid [compensation]'*.

At the same time, a convicted paedophile with a not dissimilar surname, Peter Ball, was much in the news. He too had been a bishop in the Diocese of Chichester. He was found guilty and imprisoned that same year, 2015, on numerous counts of child sexual abuse. Prior to becoming Bishop of Gloucester, he had been suffragan bishop of Lewes, part of the Diocese of Chichester. It is easy to see how the two names, Bell and Ball, from the same diocese, might be confused by the press. So we assumed that there had been a mistake, and all would be quickly sorted out.

How wrong we were.

Following the two preceding years of consideration initially by Lambeth Palace, then by a Core Group set up for the purpose in the Diocese of Chichester, the Church accepted in 2015 the complaint against Bell 'on a balance of probabilities'. It paid damages totalling

£32k – actually a fairly nominal sum, in the context of abuse cases – jointly to the complainant and her lawyer, and promptly set about ruining the reputation of the late Bishop by removing his name (and setting a precedent for others to do so) from various institutions and buildings in the Diocese of Chichester, most notably from George Bell House at 4 Canon Lane. In 2016 a new cathedral guide was published, attempting to promote confidence in the allegation.

Thence began a lengthy battle to clear the name of George Bell. What follows here is not a legal analysis, nor a claim to superior knowledge or insight by comparison with others who have been involved. Rather, as a bystander with a personal connection to the accused, I merely wanted to record my own observations on the way the Church handled the case, with which I have been greatly preoccupied for much of the past decade. I also wish to stress that I do not regard the complainant herself as in any way responsible for the Church's actions in this instance.

A considerable amount of correspondence and other unofficial documentation, published and unpublished, was accumulated in the course of a continuing struggle to clear the name of the late bishop and to restore his ruined reputation. Many people have been involved in this campaign, some far more closely and far more actively than I have. The documents at my disposal are unofficial ones. They cannot be used to scrutinise the complaint itself or the procedures that resulted in the Church's findings. Others more qualified than myself have undertaken this work. I hope their own endeavours will be published one day.

My own part has been primarily to support those who have organised meetings and other events, to participate in them whenever possible, and also to write frequent letters to the press and certain church officials. Many people have done likewise. It is not possible to quote from or even acknowledge all of them.

So because of the volume and accessibility of the paperwork my husband James and I have ourselves accumulated, and indeed sometimes ourselves generated, in both published and unpublished correspondence and papers, I have drawn only on our own records as the basis for my reflections. My original thought was it might be of particular interest to my own family and to friends and connections who have known of my concern with this case. But perhaps some of it may also now be useful to others involved in similar cases or

CHAPTER ONE In the Beginning...

with similar concerns.

My own original involvement was on account of my father, Franz Hildebrandt, who died in 1985. He was not only a close friend of Bell's, but owed the bishop a huge debt of gratitude for his personal support before and during the Second World War. My father's words speak for themselves. They contain a first-hand account of how the Bishop had helped him and so many others like him. He first wrote them in 1941 in the dedication of a *Festschrift* in Bell's honour, which he edited, and which may be one of the earliest published tributes to the late Bishop:

My dear Bishop,

The plan for this book goes back as far as November 1938. You will remember those days when we read about the pogrom in Germany, when your palace at Chichester was overflooded with letters from refugees begging you to help them to come over to England, when it became clear that not only the Jews but thousands of Christians had to leave their country. You were the first to realize their plight; you moved in the Church Assembly the setting up of a special committee for 'non-aryan' Christians and the raising of funds; and you made the start by making yourself responsible for the emigration and settlement of some forty German and Austrian theologians with their families... All of them went through internment in 1940, and it was you again who brought them out; you raised your voice in public, you went twice through all the camps on the mainland and in the Isle of Man... Today there are thousands of refugees who would wish to thank you for what you have done for them... May other readers [of this Festschrift] take it as a small witness that the universal Church of Christ is alive even in our dark times...'

(Franz Hildebrandt, *'And Other Pastors Of Thy Flock': A German Tribute To The Bishop Of Chichester*, Cambridge University Press [1942], Introduction).

My family owes its very existence to George Bell. He first became known to my father when the latter was working with his own closest friend from student days, Dietrich Bonhoeffer, in Forest Hill, south London, in 1933. Following his early return to Germany at the behest of his senior pastor Martin Niemöller, he helped to set up the Pastors' Emergency League (*der Pfarrernotbund*) and then to work in the newly formed Confessing Church (*die bekennende Kirche*). He was forced to flee back to the UK four years later (1937), after a short imprisonment in Germany, not only on account of his anti-Nazi activities but also on account of his own non-Aryan heritage.

Bell encouraged and supported him, and many others, during this refugee phase in his life. He also later intervened with Home Office officials in the autumn of 1940 to secure my father's early release – together with a number of other 'enemy alien' internees – from internment in the Isle of Man, internment which could otherwise have lasted for the duration of the Second World War. In due course this meant that my father was a free man when he met the young lady who was to become his wife (and later my mother) through a mutual friend in Cambridge in 1942; and married her a year later. Had he remained in an internment camp for the rest of the war, as happened to many others, this meeting could not have occurred.

Knowing this background to my family history and to my own life (as a small child I had gone with my parents to meet Bishop Bell myself), I could not sit silently by while the name and reputation of my father's acclaimed 'father in God' and great friend were being so badly traduced. And although it has now been publicly acknowledged that mistakes were made and that no cloud should remain over the bishop's memory, full restitution had not yet, as of the time of writing the first version of this book (December 2022), taken place. Since then, considerable progress has been made. But at the time of formal publication two years later, it still remains incomplete.

Both Bonhoeffer and my father had spent sufficient time privately with Bell to have been aware of any flaws in his character had they existed. From their time in Nazi Germany, they had good reason to be very wary of false friendships. Bell called them 'my two boys' to indicate the closeness that existed among the three of them, without any suggestion whatever of possible impropriety in their relationship. My father remained in close contact with Bell throughout the rest of the latter's life: for him, Bell was something of a father-figure (his own father having died in Germany in 1939) as well as a friend, a mentor and a counsellor. For Bell, Dietrich Bonhoeffer and Franz

Hildebrandt were perhaps akin to the sons that he and his wife Henrietta had never had.

Moreover, in the intervening years prior to the time that the complainant alleged Bell started to abuse her, the Bishop's Palace in Chichester entertained many guests, including vulnerable children from the *Kindertransport*, none of whom has ever complained of any inappropriate behaviour by the Bishop toward a single one of them. And now mature men, who had been boys in the Cathedral choir school at the actual time of the supposed abuse, who frequently encountered Bell in the Cathedral and elsewhere in the precincts but who had also personally known a genuine paedophile among the school staff, were incensed by the accusation against the Bishop and wrote a public letter to *The Times* on 6 November 2015 to say so:

> *'As former choristers at Chichester cathedral between 1949 and 1958, all of us recall [Bishop Bell] as a loved, respected and saintly figure, a bishop whom we perhaps knew better than choristers would today because back then we spent so many more weeks of the year singing services than cathedral boys do now.'*

So from the outset, the term 'balance of probabilities' to arrive at a guilty verdict would have seemed highly unlikely to anyone who had personally known, or knew anything about, Bishop Bell. None of his own family, nor close friends like Dietrich Bonhoeffer or my father, nor the wider community who knew Bell personally, would have recognised the man vilified by this case. 'Balance of improbabilities' would have been more accurate. Although not coined by me, it was a phrase that cropped up many times in various meetings and discussions. It became the starting point for this book and the title of the original unpublished version.

CHAPTER TWO
'Balance of Probabilities'

I NEED TO START by attempting to explain the legal terminology. To a layperson like myself, this has to be kept very simple, with apologies to any of my readers who hold legal qualifications or who have far greater expertise than I have. I am aware that what I have written here will appear superficial to a specialist, and that I have not dealt in any detail with certain legal areas such as the nature of evidence or standards of proof, to which I refer below. What follows is my own amateur and very general understanding of the term.

A 'balance of probabilities' is the basis on which decisions are reached in civil, as opposed to criminal, proceedings. In a criminal court, a verdict of guilt must be based on proof 'beyond reasonable doubt' that a defendant committed the crime. In civil proceedings, the required standard of proof is lower, because any penalties a civil court may impose will generally be less severe than in a criminal court. For instance, they will not normally involve lengthy prison sentences, although they could take the form of heavy fines.

But it must be established that the claimant's case is supported by the evidence presented to the court so that the so-called 'balance of probabilities' is in all likelihood weighted against the defendant. Moreover, in civil as in criminal cases, the burden of proof rests with the prosecution and not with the defence. Finally, again as in criminal cases, a presumption of innocence underlies the proceedings, unless and until the court is satisfied that the balance has tilted in the complainant's favour.

None of these criteria was applied in this case. Since the late bishop had been dead for 37 years when the accusation was first made and for almost 60 years by the time the case was settled, a criminal trial – had one been warranted – was out of the question. So, clearly, any conclusion in this instance would have to rest on a 'balance of probabilities' outcome under civil law proceedings. But a 'balance' by definition presupposes the existence of two sides to an argument. So this inevitably raises the question why a case for the defence, which would have been required in a properly constituted civil court, was never called for.

The fact that this was never even sought, let alone considered, is itself puzzling. It would not have required too much effort on the part of those concerned with handling the case to do so. A case for the defence could easily have been assembled. There were living family members and friends or relatives of those who had personally known the Bishop, his former chaplain at the time of the alleged abuse who was still alive at the time of the so-called 'investigation' and subsequent declaration of guilt, his most recent biographer who lived close at hand, and a number of other potential witnesses. Not one of these individuals was even informed of the impending proceedings, far less invited to participate in them. Secrecy seems to have been integral to the entire process. With hindsight, there may actually have been fear of a possible defence.

It has already been suggested that a 'balance of probabilities' verdict was in fact a highly improbable one. The lack of consultation attests this improbability. Had there been any effort to contact some of the above-mentioned individuals, it should have been immediately obvious that the allegation was highly dubious from the outset, for a variety of reasons that subsequently came to light in the course of Lord Carlile's review of 2017.

This should have led to more, rather than less, investigation. Lip service was paid at the time, by some of those prosecuting the case, to the late Bishop's reputation. But it was always qualified by phrases such as 'good men are capable of bad deeds', and therefore dismissed as being irrelevant. Bell's reputation should have been sufficient reason in itself for a thorough and impartial investigation, as noted in a private letter to me from a canon in another diocese, who knows Chichester well:

> *'The action of the diocese of Chichester has all the qualities of a knee-jerk reaction, by a diocese which has an appalling record in safeguarding. Sadly, Bishop Bell's reputation has suffered as a result of Chichester's recent history.' (21 November 2017).*

CHAPTER TWO 'Balance of Probabilities'

Given that the late George Bell was one of the greatest Anglican bishops of the 20th century and as close to being called a saint as is possible in the Protestant church (he is commemorated in the Church of England calendar on the anniversary of his death on 3 October every year), this lack of investigation is all the more questionable. It appears that his public image, including among many other considerations his courageous stand against Nazism on the one hand and his opposition to the blanket bombing of civilian centres in Germany on the other, not to mention his own humanitarian work with refugees already noted in the Introduction, did not merit consideration. The same correspondent writes:

'I remember as a teenager, my late father (not a church goer) telling me of Bishop Bell standing up in the House of Lords to condemn the indiscriminate bombing of German cities. Bishop Bell was vilified by many for speaking out at the time. History now sees his words as prophetic. My father was impressed by his courage' (ibid).

In fact, as we shall see, Bell's exemplary character and his selfless actions seemed to have counted against him and to have been used as an excuse to cast doubt on his innocence, rather than as a reason to investigate the allegation properly.

The wrong lessons seem to have been learned from the Jimmy Savile case, which broke in 2012, and which the police were accused in 2013 of not investigating properly because of his celebrity status. This may have had some repercussions for the case of George Bell, which was first referred to Lambeth Palace at exactly the same time. More will be said about this below.

CHAPTER THREE
The Context: Surge of Suspicion

AS ALREADY NOTED, any properly constituted court in this country should uphold the principle underlying civil law, as in criminal law, that a person is presumed to be innocent until proven guilty. Accordingly, I weighed into the publicity that the case had already generated with my own first letter to the press on the subject, as follows:

> '...I am deeply saddened by the recent accusations against the bishop. However, like Charles Moore (Church Times, Comment, 2 January 2016), I am even more saddened by the Church's apparent willingness to ignore the basic principle of British justice: that a person is innocent until proven guilty. It would appear that the primary motivation in the Church's decision to compensate the alleged victim and disgrace Bishop Bell was fear of public outcry had it not done so...' (Church Times, 5 January 2016)

At that stage I had not registered the fact that the Church itself admitted that the process that had resulted in Bell's condemnation had not taken place in a properly constituted court of law. This admission was publicised sometime later in the revised and discreditable cathedral guide of 2016. From the outset, I was merely trying to understand the basis on which such an improbable decision had been made. The 'fear of public outcry' needed some investigation.

It is hard to isolate the George Bell case from its wider context. It is a highly regrettable fact that while child sexual abuse is known to have been carried out by a significant number of clergy in the Church of England, as in other denominations and institutions, in the past – and still continues to this day – the reputation of the Diocese of Chichester has historically been particularly bad in this regard. The aforementioned Peter Ball was only one of a number of actual perpetrators in the area. As already noted with regard to the choirboys who had known the Bishop, there was at least one case in Bell's own time of paedophilia among the staff of the cathedral school itself. The recent Independent Inquiry into Child Sexual Abuse (IICSA) hearings of 2018 devoted a whole session to Chichester alone. Even before the allegation against George Bell was brought to the attention of Archbishop Welby and thence sent to Bishop Warner, the scale of the problem had prompted the first Archiepiscopal Visitation (under Archbishop Williams) to the diocese for 120 years. The earlier Carmi (2004), Meekings (2009), and Butler-Sloss (2011) reports had all drawn attention to the existence and extent of abuse in the area.

In addition, the Jimmy Savile scandal, which broke in 2012, helped to encourage many victims of child sexual abuse throughout the country and from a wide variety of institutions and organisations in the UK to come forward with their (often retrospective) accounts of their own experiences at the hands of numerous paedophiles, contributing to the so-called #MeToo campaign here. While many of these have indeed been upheld on subsequent investigation, it does need to be noted that not all have been genuine allegations. Some of the most notorious were investigated by Operation Yewtree in 2012–13, involving claims against a number of VIPs. Cases against such individuals as Gary Glitter resulted in convictions. But several others – specifically against Sir Cliff Richard, Paul Gambaccini, and Neil Fox – were later proven false. This investigation took place amid great publicity, and, like the Savile case, coincided with the time that George Bell's alleged victim contacted Archbishop Welby.

There followed the allegations made by Carl Beech or 'Nick' between 2014 and 2016 against still more VIPs, including MPs and high-ranking army officers. They were finally disproved through Operation Midland in 2019, culminating in the Henriques Report and in Beech's conviction and imprisonment. But this did not occur before a number of reputations, not to mention the entire lives of innocent people and their families, had been ruined. Lord Brittan, one of those falsely accused, died without knowing that his name had been cleared. The cavalier attitude demonstrated by some investigators, such as that of the ITV journalist whose work in 2012

CHAPTER THREE   The Context: Surge of Suspicion

resulted in the exposure of Jimmy Savile, reflects the general lack of concern in the media for such victims. He commented that:

> *'it must be very difficult for [innocent defendants] to objectively see "the bigger picture" of bringing the guilty to book.'* ('The Accused: National Treasures on Trial', Channel 4, 24 August 2022).

Yes, it would be difficult to see the 'bigger picture' when someone is driven, as has happened with many falsely accused individuals, to the depths of despair, professional ruin, and social ostracisation. In at least one known instance among the clergy alone, it has resulted in suicide.

There is another factor to be considered. In the mid-1990s, about the time that the complainant 'Carol' in the George Bell affair first brought her allegation to the attention of the then Bishop of Chichester, Eric Kemp, the so-called 'recovered memory' approach was much in the news. This was a therapy popular among many practitioners at the time and still continues to be in use, although it is far from universally accepted. Patients were encouraged to recall memories of traumatic events in their childhood, particularly sexual abuse, in order to explain certain kinds of dysfunctional behaviour and other difficulties in their lives and relationships in later years. However, it was argued that many such memories were imaginary rather than real, and the process has subsequently been discredited by many professionals.

The George Bell case may be a possible example of 'recovered memory' on the part of the claimant. Professor Tony Maden, a psychiatrist who examined the complainant in Lord Carlile's review of the case, noted that

> *...memory is not reliable over such long periods of time; [and] "false memory" could not be ruled out in this instance... There are enormous problems for the expert arising from the fact that the Claimant is now assessed 63 years after the material events... Recall is an active mental process in which memories tend to become distorted with time to fit the individual's beliefs, needs and values... Events can and do acquire a significance years later that they did not have at the time.* (Carlile Report, 15 December 2017.)

Professor Maden does not comment on the still extant tendency of many professionals to favour the 'recovered memory' approach to explain past traumas and psychological problems, and this excerpt is not to be taken as indicative of his own opinion about such a trend one way or the other. But insofar as the wider context as manifested in counselling techniques and therapies of the 1990s and following years may possibly have provided an impetus to 'Carol's' complaint against George Bell, it needs to be noted as part of the background to the various events of the next decade or so mentioned above.

That all this was occurring simultaneously with the George Bell case is striking. While it does not excuse the way in which the Church authorities handled the matter and the gross miscarriage of justice that ensued, it may perhaps help us to understand how it all arose by putting it in a more general historical and societal context. There can be little doubt that those authorities felt – and indeed still feel – under great pressure to be seen to take the side of an alleged victim of abuse, in this instance as in others. It was revealing that a letter from Rt The Rev Martin Warner, current Bishop of Chichester, coincidentally appeared next to mine in the same issue of the *Church Times* in January 2016:

> '...*Within Britain, and certainly within the Church of England, we are seeking to move on from a culture in which manipulation of power meant that victims were too afraid to make allegations, or allegations were easily dismissed...*'

Another trend was developing at the same time. Since the turn of the millennium, the infamous Soham murders and the subsequent growth of a safeguarding culture throughout society as a whole and the Church in particular, an underlying atmosphere of distrust has been increasing in this country and elsewhere throughout society at large. Any individual in any position that might bring him or her into contact with children or 'vulnerable people', however peripherally and whether in a paid or voluntary capacity, is required to submit to Disclosure and Barring Service (DBS, formerly CRB [Criminal Records Bureau]) checks, and attend regular safeguarding courses. These now seem to be of greater importance in many churches than regular religious observances. As has been observed by others in a number of columns, the safeguarding officer in a church today sometimes seems to be held in as much regard nowadays as a priest, if not more so.

While church attendance itself is not compulsory (although it is obviously expected) for church workers, attendance at safeguarding courses is now required in most mainstream Christian denominations, not just in the Church of England. Thus safeguarding considerations are in some respects taking precedence over, and may indeed be undermining, the church's role in providing many services and activities. They are certainly influencing congregational attitudes and are having a negative impact on the willingness of some to volunteer for any type of church work. One notable example, in 2010, was the resignation *en masse* of a group of flower-arranging ladies of Gloucester Cathedral in protest over a sacking of one of their number for refusing to submit to CRB checks, lest she might encounter any of the choirboys in the course of fulfilling her duties.

The emphasis on safeguarding is helping to fuel this climate of misgiving in the church, as in our wider society. For an institution whose entire *raison d'etre* is that of faith and trust, it is a lamentable state of affairs. And yet, despite it all, abuse continues to be perpetrated by some of those who have supposedly been cleared by the process. The current Soul Survivor case is one example. A CRB or DBS check is only as good as the day on which it is carried out. It was reported (October 2022) that almost 400 new abuse cases had been discovered in the latest Past Cases Review undertaken by the National Safeguarding Steering Group of the Church of England. Although some of these date well back into the last century, of which the John Smyth affair is a notorious example, many have occurred since CRB checks were first introduced in 2002.

The combination of such checks and safeguarding considerations is arguably playing a part in bringing about a different approach to many disciplinary and legal processes in the church and in other institutions. No longer is one innocent until proven guilty. Now, a person may be deemed guilty until proven innocent, as was perhaps illustrated by the sacking of the Gloucester cathedral volunteer. He or she is required to submit to regular DBS checks in order to demonstrate innocence and suitability for a particular role. Failure to comply may deem the individual concerned as unsuitable, and is likely to result in the non-issuing or termination of contracts or voluntary agreements. While there are certainly a number of roles in a church for which a DBS check may be justified, such as those involving direct contact with children or vulnerable people, there are many others (coffee rotas, adult choir membership, flower arranging and so on) for which it is less demonstrably so. It may indeed be fostering an atmosphere of distrust which is counterproductive in any church. Any further measures that may be introduced in an attempt to make churches 'safer' as a result of the Makin report need to be very carefully considered in this light.

From this point, it is only a small step for a presumption of guilt to become the basis for judging all church workers, clergy or lay, paid or unpaid. This helps lay the foundation for the way in which many instances involving safeguarding in general and child sexual abuse in particular are handled. In far too many instances similar to that of Bishop Bell, there has been an immediate knee-jerk reaction in recent years in support of those who have brought – and continue to bring – accusations of abuse against individual members of the clergy. Such accusations have resulted in the instant suspension of the accused, and the removal of permission to officiate even on one-off occasions in their own churches or elsewhere, sometimes before an actual investigation is begun. (Moreover, in at least one case this was imposed on a cleric by a bishop who was himself rumoured to be under police investigation, a case subsequently abandoned owing only to a lapse of time in its pursuit). Thus a cloud of suspicion is created over the accused. And indeed an eventual 'innocent' verdict may never completely succeed in removing it. This is certainly true for a number of clergy in our own time. It is also indubitably part of the growing undercurrent of unease within the Church in general, and the diocese of Chichester in particular, that preceded the George Bell affair.

CHAPTER FOUR
Case? What Case?

Not a Court of Law

SO RIGHT FROM the start, the lines in this dispute were drawn. On the side of family, friends and supporters of the late Bishop, who knew nothing about the case until it was over, was the underlying presumption of innocence. On the other, by the Church authorities charged with handling the affair, there had been an immediate presumption of guilt. It is not surprising that this was felt by so many people to have been a 'knee-jerk' reaction to a single allegation. The question that must be answered is why the authorities reacted to it and dealt with it in the way they did, ignoring the procedures that should have brought the case openly to a civil court.

There are several possible reasons for this. That of political expediency has already been mentioned. The government at the time was known to be committed to a public enquiry into sexual abuse in the Church and in other institutions; and possibly diocesan officials wished to get ahead of the game by turning the spotlight on one of their own. IICSA had been set up the previous year (2014), two years after the Archiepiscopal Visitation to Chichester instigated by Archbishop Rowan Williams that had been prompted by the many known cases of child sexual abuse occurring among clergy in the diocese in previous years. To turn one of the Church's own most sainted leaders into a sacrificial lamb was perhaps seen as a way of scoring brownie points among genuine abuse victims as well as in the wider world. One long since dead, who could not answer for himself and who also could not personally suffer from the process, at least in his own lifetime, would be an ideal victim.

Moreover, the Church authorities must have known they could not win in open court, without a case for the defence being presented or even requested. With a basic presumption of innocence – whether in a civil or criminal case – it is for the prosecution to prove guilt. With a presumption of guilt, based on an unsubstantiated allegation, it is much easier for those prosecuting the case to achieve the desired outcome. The witch trials of previous centuries spring to mind here. The fact that the late Bishop was no longer alive to defend himself should have been all the more reason for a wider circle of family, friends and associates to be consulted. That they were not consulted speaks reams in itself. Just as with the secrecy surrounding the whole affair, it suggests that the team handling the allegation may privately have had cause to believe that it could not be upheld, and indeed might actually have been disproved, had it been publicised from the outset.

The secrecy continued, even after the shock announcement of October 2015. Repeated requests to reveal the sources of evidence used in the case were refused. On 15 April 2016 I wrote to ask Bishop Warner:

> 'when are you going to allow the evidence contained in the recent review of the Bell case to be heard in public?'

He replied on 22 April 2016 that *'the information you request is not withheld by the Church by* [sic] *its own; we are constrained by law from disclosing that information'*.

I tried again:

> '…I am baffled by your response that you "are constrained by law from disclosing that information". Since the review has not yet been incorporated in a legal process of any kind, I do not understand why any kind of legal constraint is applicable here, or what that constraint could possibly be. Moreover, if the diocese committed itself to silence as part of the agreement reached with the complainant, that still does not prevent me and others from asking why this was the case, and to question whether the fact that she has since made a public statement may actually now render such an agreement null and void.' (3 May 2016).

And I received this reply back from Bishop Warner almost immediately:

> 'Thank you for your response. To clarify, the advice from our lawyers is that we are bound by the law that governs the settle-

ment of a civil case.' (5 May 2016)

But there had been no civil case to be settled. This did not answer the questions I had asked, so having consulted (through my husband James) with a former university colleague and senior legal expert who himself had served prior to his retirement as chancellor of another diocese, I wrote again to Bishop Warner again on 11 May 2016:

'I would like specific answers to the following points, on which I have taken advice:

- *A diocesan "committee", such as that set up to investigate the Bell case, has no status as a court. It may use the procedures of a civil law court, but these cannot be held to indicate that a legal process has been duly carried out.*

- *"Carol's" subsequent interviews with the media abrogate any confidentiality agreements that may have been reached between the two parties in settlement of the case.*

- *In any case in law where claims have been made against one party, it is incumbent upon lawyers to obtain statements from both parties. This is especially the case where the accused is long dead. I have been advised that it would not be possible to come to a legally valid decision if this has not happened. Moreover, it is not permissible for one party (i.e. the Diocese of Chichester) to act as judge and jury in a case in which it has an interest.*

- *A case for the defence has now been assembled by the George Bell Support Group, containing evidence (including an eyewitness account) that has not yet been tested in court. It is now incumbent on the Diocese to reopen the case and place a new investigation in the hands of the appropriate impartial and legally recognised authorities.'*

This letter elicited no response at all.

By not replying to letters, or replying in words that did not answer the questions posed, it was becoming apparent that no further information on the case would be forthcoming from those who had been concerned with determining its outcome. In his address to the

'Rebuilding Bridges' meeting in Chichester on 4 February 2019 organised by Richard Symonds, Bishop Warner publicly stated that *'Bishop Bell cannot be proven guilty'*. This was a very equivocal phrase, and fell far short of the outright declaration of innocence that should have been made. Instead, the bishop noted that there remained in some circles a continuing belief in Bell's guilt, even after both the Carlile and the Briden reports (as Warner acknowledged) had found to the contrary. More will be said below about these two reports.

The Reputation Trap

So why did the Church authorities think that there might have been grounds for upholding an unsubstantiated posthumous accusation of child sexual abuse? One reason already mentioned was the very fact of the late Bishop's impeccable reputation and international standing, as Bishop Warner hinted in his *Church Times* letter of January 2016. Ten days after that letter was published, this comment by Gabrielle Higgins, secretary to the Diocese of Chichester, appeared in the *Church Times* under the headline 'No one should be above suspicion':

> *'We must never demand a higher threshold of suspicion because the accused person is of high standing, however uncomfortable this may make us feel.' (Church Times, 15 January 2016).*

My husband, James Grayson, promptly replied:

> *'The Diocesan Secretary of Chichester is mistaken in her assertion that critics of the actions of the diocese in the case of the late Bishop George Bell were arguing that he should be above suspicion. I know of no one who has made that argument. The questions that were raised have to do with the complete secrecy surrounding the announcement [October 2015]. There was no intimation that Bishop Bell was under investigation: only a guilty verdict was announced – and a defenceless person's reputation was trashed' (Church Times, 29 January 2016).*

This was yet another letter which elicited no further comment from the Church.

In the opening sentences of my previously quoted letter to Bishop Warner on 3 May 2016, I observed:

> 'As has repeatedly been stated in the press, no one is saying that Bishop Bell was above the law. What has been stated over and over again is that under the law of this land, a person is deemed to be innocent until proven guilty. There is as yet no element of proof in this case, and there cannot be until both sides of the argument have been duly and openly heard in court.'

Certainly, Bell's illustrious and impeccable reputation was a major reason why there was such a widespread and sustained outcry against the Church's guilty verdict. But that is not to say that the case should never have been investigated. On the contrary, it should have been all the more reason for a careful, thorough and impartial investigation. Lord Carlile discusses this in his report on the case (*Lord Carlile of Berriew, CBE, QC, Bishop George Bell: The Independent Review,* 15 December 2017 [online]). He notes that it was his very reputation that had resulted in such an outcry against the 'balance of probabilities' verdict, and concludes that

> 'For Bishop Bell's reputation to be catastrophically affected in the way that occurred was just wrong' *(para. 268).*

Another correspondent wrote to me in a private letter on 24 March 2016:

> 'Not that [George Bell's] public reputation must protect him from any evidence of private wrong-doing, but it ought to mean that allegations should be properly investigated before they are accepted as true.'

But it was the Church, not the majority of Bell supporters, that cited his reputation as an excuse not to investigate the case properly. We were constantly being reminded that 'good men are capable of evil deeds', as if that was enough to defend the Church's position. In a further attempt to justify the diocesan stand on the matter, Ms Higgins was at pains to point out in that same *Church Times* article that

> '...there is no doubt that George Bell achieved many great things during his lifetime, for which he is rightly honoured and which continue to be remembered'.

Thus the diocese sought to pay lip service to the very reputation they sought to demolish, indicating perhaps that there was a great deal of ambivalence among them as to the conclusion they had reached. Another correspondent wrote back to the same paper:

> 'Why, then, is the diocese attempting to erase his memory by renaming its guest house, which had previously been known as George Bell House? It was presumably named after Bishop Bell in recognition of the many great things he achieved during his lifetime' (Roy Sully, Church Times, 29 January 2016).

The words used by Archbishop Rowan Williams in dedicating the building in October 2008, quoted later in Chapter 6, confirm this.

Right from the beginning, the Diocese of Chichester seems to have been trying to have it both ways, possibly reflecting the aforementioned political and social pressures it was under on numerous fronts. Separating the man from the deeds was a recurrent theme in the 'official' argument over the next few years. But could anyone who genuinely believed Bell was a paedophile have taken such an equivocal stand?

Any initial ambivalence on the part of diocesan officials was well concealed by the attempt to justify the lack of adherence to normal legal procedures in the eyes of the public. During the months following the announcement of October 2015, the Cathedral authorities proceeded to publish a new guide to the building. In the section relating to George Bell, this stated that the judgment, *'although not tested in a court of law, was plausible'* (2016). Both paid and volunteer cathedral staff were admonished to make no reference to Bell unless there were direct queries about him.

Lack of Evidence = Evidence

Next, it seems that in a situation where there was absolutely no evidence to support the allegation against George Bell, the lack of evidence itself was used to defend the finding against him. This is demonstrated by correspondence between Gabrielle Higgins and James in the late summer of 2016. Here are some excerpts:

From James to Ms Higgins (27 August 2016):

> 'I regret to say that you have not actually answered the question… on what basis the case against the late Bishop Bell was made…
>
> 'My concern with the case made against Bishop Bell has been

CHAPTER FOUR Case? What Case?

twofold:

1. that there was no public announcement that an allegation had been made against him and that this allegation would be investigated. The public was only informed about the outcome of the investigation.

2. that little or no investigation appears to have been made into Bishop Bell's own circumstances at the time. It is known that (a) persons directly connected with Bishop Bell at the time were not consulted, such as his chaplain, members of his family, and others; (b) his biographer, who is resident in Chichester, was not consulted for advice about sources or indeed his opinion about the case; (c) his documents held in Lambeth Palace, including his diaries, were not consulted.'

This last point provoked the response from Ms Higgins (2 September 2016) that

'I don't think it would risk disclosure of [the complainant's] identity to confirm that the documents held in Lambeth Palace were in fact consulted, but the nature of them was not such as to be capable of casting light on the matter one way or another'.

In turn James responded (5 September 2016):

'...I presume by this you mean that nothing was found in them which corroborated the accusation made against Bishop Bell... I would like to reiterate my question: what types of sources were used to corroborate the accusation?'

This elicited the further reply on 6 September 2016 from Ms Higgins that

'...nothing was found [in the Bell papers] which corroborated the accusation and <u>nothing was found which undermined it</u>' [her emphasis]

This statement shows the absurdity of the Church's position. Bell was apparently deemed guilty because he had not himself recorded a statement of denial against the possibility of an accusation being made decades later. Did the authorities seriously expect to find among the Bell papers, or any other records detailing his life and work, evidence that he had *not* abused a child between 1948 and

1951, just in case anyone should accuse him of having done so half a century later? As Andrew Chandler, Bell's most recent biographer, had written in the *Church Times* several months previously:

> '...if innocence, not guilt, must be proved, how may any innocent man or woman feel safe, particularly when an accusation may be made... decades later, with no necessity to prove things in court, no need for conventional proof, little consistency, and no corroboration?' (Church Times, 20 May 2016)

Those concerned might do well to reflect on the fact that those controversial DBS checks, so ingrained in Church procedures today for vetting officers and workers, depend on an underlying assumption that lack of evidence will be taken as proof of innocence, not of guilt. Otherwise, there would be no church workers at all nowadays, whether paid or voluntary. That would of course include staff in the Diocese of Chichester.

Believing the Complainant

But Ms Higgins, in common with other colleagues in the Church, did not accept this in George Bell's case. The lack of evidence in itself became an additional reason to believe the complainant. In 2018 Colin Perkins, then safeguarding officer for the Diocese of Chichester, stated at the IICSA enquiry into a catalogue of abuse within the Diocese in more recent years that

> 'the typical account is a sole complainant who can offer nothing but their own account. If we are to disbelieve that person, then we are to disbelieve the typical complainant' (Independent Inquiry into Child Sexual Abuse, Diocese of Chichester, 2018).

A perceived obligation to accept an unsubstantiated allegation has thus become a basis for a guilty verdict. Perkins failed to draw the necessary distinction between believing a complainant outright and taking her (or him) seriously. The latter, not the former, would have been the correct course of action.

Perkins was not alone in this. A precedent had already been set by police investigations into other ongoing high profile abuse cases. The Church undoubtedly had a duty of pastoral care to the complainant, which the former Bishop, Eric Kemp, had actually tried – albeit misguidedly – to fulfil by arranging counselling for her in the first instance rather than referring the complaint to the appropriate authorities. But pastoral care should not presuppose complete acceptance of the veracity of a complaint from the outset. Rather, such a complaint necessitates a close and thorough investigation of the matter by an independent third party. Again, that 'independent third party' was completely lacking in the George Bell case. So by virtue of having a hitherto untarnished reputation, and also of having neglected to record in his own diaries or papers a statement that he had *not* committed any offence of which he might later be accused, he was deemed guilty – with no opportunity for a defence – by a group of people who did not themselves constitute a court of law and who had no intention of referring the case to such a court.

We have already noted that in civil law, under which the case was allegedly adjudicated, the level of proof required for a guilty verdict may be somewhat lower than in criminal cases. Nevertheless, there does have to be some level of proof. But proof in any form was completely lacking in this instance – unless, of course, the fact that an allegation existed was deemed to be proof in itself. This will be explored further below.

CHAPTER FIVE
From Incredulity ... To Fury

The Carlile Report

MEANWHILE, SUPPORTERS of George Bell were keeping up the pressure. The spate of private correspondence, as well as letters to the press, continued. Prof Andrew Chandler, Desmond Browne KC and other members of the George Bell Group convened by Chandler were particularly active in seeking and collecting relevant statements. Eventually, in June 2016, the Church of England announced that *'it would be undertaking an independent review into how the case was managed and the key processes involved in the decision-making'* (Carlile Report, 2017).

Yet it took a further five months for this request to be conveyed to Lord Carlile (November 2016). In the meantime a petition launched by another leading campaigner, Richard Symonds, was handed in to Lambeth Palace in October 2016 with over 2000 signatures, calling for the case to be reopened *'in light of the fact that a strong case for the late bishop's defence has now been assembled by a number of people with close connections to him'* (*Daily Telegraph*, 15 October 2016).

However, the case itself was not reopened. When he eventually received his brief, Lord Carlile's remit was very limited. He was specifically asked to 'conduct a Review into the way the Church of England dealt with a complaint of sexual abuse made by a woman known as "Carol" against the late Bishop Bell' (Carlile Report, *ibid.*). He was not asked to conduct a review into the actual case itself. This could, as indeed it did, lead to speculation that the Church had reason to be concerned that the case had been far from watertight in the first place and would not stand close scrutiny by an eminent lawyer.

Lord Carlile's well publicised review took place from November 2016 and throughout much of the following year. His findings, published online in December 2017, include *inter alia* the following comments in his report:

> '11. I have concluded that the Church of England acted throughout in good faith. It was motivated by a desire to do what it perceived to be the right thing by the complainant.'

> '12. Its actions were informed by history in which the Church has been, at best, slow to acknowledge abuse by its clergy and, at worst, believed to have turned a blind eye.'

> '13. I have concluded that the process followed by the Church in this case was deficient in a number of respects.'

> '14. The most significant was that the Core Group which it established failed to follow a process that was fair and equitable to both sides.'

> '18. ...The Church, understandably concerned not to repeat the mistakes of the past when it had been too slow to recognise that abuse had been perpetrated by clergy and to recognise the pain and damage caused to victims, has in effect oversteered in this case. In other words, there was a rush to judgement: the Church, feeling it should be both supportive of the complainant and transparent in its dealings, failed to engage in a process which would also give proper consideration to the rights of the Bishop. Such rights should not be treated as having been extinguished on death.'

> '26. ....It should be made clear to complainants that their complaints are not considered to be proved until findings of fact have been made...'

The report was received by the relevant Church authorities in October 2017, but it took another two months for it to be published. Lord Carlile not only found that the process had been highly flawed; he wrote that he had found no evidence to substantiate the allegation in the course of his own inquiries. It speaks for itself that Lord Carlile's remit stopped short of a request to re-examine the actual case, but was to be concerned only with the process. It is impossible to avoid the conclusion that this was because there was no case to investigate. As Lord Carlile states in paragraph 17:

> 'Where, as in this case, it is clear that the Crown Prosecution Service evidential charging standard (a realistic prospect of conviction) would not have been met, that should be a material consideration in the case.'

The Church did publicly state that it agreed with most of the report's findings, the main one of which was that it had indeed handled the matter badly. It apologised for that. The only finding with which those concerned immediately disagreed was that relating to the anonymity of the accused. They argued that naming a defendant in the early stages of an investigation might encourage more complainants to come forward, as has happened in other cases, most notably like those of Jimmy Savile and – more recently – of Mohammed al Fayed, neither of which involved the Church.

But in view of the fact that the entire case was concluded before it was made public, the validity or otherwise of such an argument was of questionable relevance in this instance. This could be another example of the authorities' fear that publicising the allegation might actually have been counterproductive from their point of view. Instead of leading to more complainants coming forward, it is more than likely to have resulted in the demolition of the case from the outset by the assembling and presentation of a credible defence.

Indeed, when Lord Carlile instituted his own public appeal for evidence at the start of his investigation, no reliable witnesses responded to support any allegations of abuse. On the contrary, a witness (now living abroad) contacted him to say that she had frequently been in the Bishop's palace in Chichester at the time of the alleged abuse and had never seen the complainant. So just as it is likely that calling for a defence would have resulted in the abandonment of the case, it is also quite likely that had the Church authorities actually publicised the lone allegation against George Bell at the time it was made, they could have saved themselves the trouble and expense – and eventual embarrassment – of pursuing it any further.

Following the delayed publication of the Carlile Report, it was anticipated by Bell's supporters that this would be the end of the matter. However, instead of issuing an outright statement that there had been a miscarriage of justice and immediately moving to restore Bell's reputation and the various named memorials to him in Chichester and elsewhere, the Church proceeded to make matters worse. That same day (15 December 2017), Archbishop Welby declared that

> 'a significant cloud is left over [Bell's] name' and that while he 'was in many ways a hero, he is also accused of great wickedness. No human being is entirely good or bad'. He went on to add the now familiar catchphrase that 'good acts do not diminish evil ones'.

On 18 December 2017 I wrote to the Archbishop as follows:

> '…The findings of the [Carlile] report have confirmed that the Church's handling of this case was deficient, unprofessional, and improper throughout. In view of the fact that the late Bishop's guilt has not been, and cannot be, proved (nor was it Lord Carlile's remit to do so), it follows that George Bell is innocent of the charge brought against him… Your statement in response to the Carlile Report that "good acts do not diminish evil ones" is a feeble attempt to defend the Church's actions. The "evil act" in this case has been the behaviour of all those involved in bringing the charge against George Bell and in acting indefensibly in the way the case was handled and decided.'

Needless to say, I received no reply to this letter, nor to one I sent at the same time along similar lines to Bishop Warner. No surprises there. I had not expected one.

Further Allegations and the Briden Report

Much anger was expressed in the media following the Archbishop's 'significant cloud' statement. In view of the Church's apparent acceptance of Lord Carlile's overall opinion – that there had been no case to answer – it made no sense at all. However, in response to the ensuing fury expressed by many individuals in the press and especially by open letters to Lambeth Palace by groups of professional historians, theologians, and judges, the archbishop sought to justify his remark in a statement quoted by the *Daily Telegraph* on 23 January 2018, that *'I cannot with integrity rescind my statement'*.

This served to reinforce the argument that the mere existence of an allegation was regarded as proof of guilt in itself.

Almost as if to support this stand, the Church produced – out of the blue – a second set of allegations, conveniently timed to detract attention from the Carlile report and to pre-empt both any moves toward restitution and a discussion of the case at General Synod in February 2018. These allegations mainly centred on those made by another lady in her 70s called 'Alison', who claimed to have been sexually assaulted in 1949 at the age of nine by Bishop Bell. There was also a complaint by an 80-year-old man, stating that his mother had told him she had seen George Bell committing a sexual act with a man on the bonnet of his Rolls-Royce in 1967. Not only had Bell never had a Rolls-Royce: he had also been dead for nine years by the time of this alleged offence.

Whether these allegations had already been made earlier in the autumn is unclear. And if they were genuine, why were they not made to Lord Carlile the previous year, at the time of his public call for evidence and witnesses? The fact that they had not been disclosed sooner does seem to suggest that their release was being saved for a time when they would be most damaging to the growing campaign for justice for George Bell. Moreover, Welby's infamous 'significant cloud' remark also seemed to indicate that he had prior knowledge of it before the Carlile report was published.

It beggars belief that these complaints could be taken seriously by the Church. It further beggars belief that they were deemed credible enough to be referred in the first instance to West Sussex police and then, when the police found there was no case to answer, to yet another internal investigation, in 2018. If there had been incredulity at the announcement in October 2015 that Bell had been found 'on balance' to have been guilty of the initial allegation, that incredulity was completely dwarfed by the fury that greeted news of the subsequent allegations. The anger was not only rife among those who had campaigned all along for 'Justice for Bell', but was echoed by the words of Lord Carlile himself, in the following statement:

'I think it was unwise, unnecessary and foolish to issue a press release in relation to something that remains to be investigated and which was not part of the material placed before me over the period of more than a year in which I carried out my review.

> *During that period the review was well known, and it was open to anybody to place information before me.'* (*Daily Telegraph,* 1 February 2018)

Andrew Chandler described the announcement as 'shameful', a sentiment echoed by many other correspondents. Its timing was also suspect. In the same edition, the *Daily Telegraph* noted that the Church of England was about to debate, at its synod the following day, the handling of the George Bell matter amid calls for Archbishop Welby's resignation. It is almost certain that the Church had known of the matter for some time previously. The synod debate never took place. Neither, on that occasion, was the archbishop formally asked to resign.

Other individuals continued to write to the press in a professional as well as a personal capacity. Such activity continued apace well into 2018. One persistent correspondent for several years was His Honour Anthony Nicholl. An example of his stand is illustrated by his reference to *'the astonishing disregard for the law of the land, by... the diocese of Chichester'* (*Daily Telegraph,* 31 March 2018). This was echoed in the letters of many other correspondents.

A Core Group was reassembled by the diocese of Chichester to consider the new allegations, indicating that little had been learned from the Carlile Report regarding the necessity of independent investigation. And another of the most fundamental mistakes that had caused Lord Carlile to criticise their earlier proceedings was repeated. Although a lawyer for the defence was eventually appointed this time, it was initially by the Core Group and not by the family. Considerable pressure was brought to bear on the authorities by Andrew Chandler to allow Desmond Browne KC to assemble and present an independent case for the defence on behalf of Mrs Barbara Whitley, the late bishop's sole surviving niece (who subsequently died in October 2020).

The senior ecclesiastical lawyer appointed by the diocese to review the new claims was Timothy Briden KC. His report may be found online: *In The Matter Of The Late George Bell, And In The Matter Of An Investigation Before The Right Worshipful Timothy Briden, Commissary Of The Bishop Of Chichester* (July 2018). Like Lord Carlile in 'Carol's' case, he declared the new allegations to be unfounded, saying of 'Alison's' complaints that her evidence was similar enough to that of the first complainant 'Carol' to be a copycat imitation made

> 'to support Carol and those who have upheld the validity of Carol's complaint... My conclusion [is] that Alison's evidence is unreliable and incapable of supporting any adverse finding against Bishop Bell' (p.8).'

'Alison's' claim was found to have been inconsistent between her oral and written statements. And Mr Briden wrote of the second complainant: *'I have no hesitation in rejecting the "hearsay statement" of [his] mother'* (p.11).

Like Lord Carlile, Mr Briden acknowledged Bell's outstanding character, while stating that this had not influenced the outcome of the case:

> 'For some witnesses... it is inconceivable that a person of Bishop Bell's faith and integrity should have been guilty of abusive behaviour... A closer examination of Bishop Bell's attitudes, beliefs and lifestyle might have become necessary had the case against him... been credible following investigation. It was not.' (p.14)

Because the allegations were so patently defective, there must be grounds for thinking that following the negative findings of the Carlile Report, the Church authorities were desperate to secure a guilty verdict this time. Reasons as to why this might be so are discussed in the concluding chapter.

Guilty by Allegation

It appeared that the entire case for the prosecution rested on nothing more than unsubstantiated and increasingly unbelievable allegations. Following the Carlile report, the mere existence of an allegation was apparently enough to justify the Church's stand, as Justin Welby's 'significant cloud' remark exemplified. It seems that this was the only negative thing that could be said against George Bell. Given that the authorities seemed by then to be reluctantly accepting that Bell could not be proven guilty, the fact that an allegation had been made was now being used as evidence in itself of wrongdoing.

Over time, however, a change in attitude began to appear. The continued pressure from George Bell supporters was perhaps finally being felt. In a statement issued by Lambeth Palace on 24 January 2019, subsequent to the publication of the Briden report, Archbishop Welby said:

> *'I apologise profoundly and unconditionally for the hurt caused [to vast numbers of people] by the failures in parts of the process and take responsibility for this failure. However, it is still the case that there is a woman who came forward with a serious allegation relating to an historic case of abuse and this cannot be ignored or swept under the carpet. We need to care for her and listen to her voice.'*

With these words, the Archbishop seemed to acknowledge that there was a difference between believing a complainant outright, as had initially happened in this case and continued to be advocated by diocesan officers in Chichester, and the need to take her complaint seriously. There is a marked modification in his tone here, by comparison with his 'significant cloud' statement just 12 months earlier.

By this time, of course, reports into other cases in which miscarriages of justice were demonstrated were being publicised. In 2018, Sir Cliff Richard, an avowed Christian, received £2m in settlement of his case against the BBC, a sum which it is not inconceivable that George Bell could have claimed against the Diocese of Chichester had he been alive. And within a few months of Welby's more moderate words in January 2019, the Henriques Report on Operation Midland (the Carl Beech affair) was published. It was becoming clear that not all allegations of sexual abuse were credible ones.

But there was still some way to go before Archbishop Welby eventually apologised for his late retraction of the damaging 'significant cloud' statement of January 2018. That took almost another four years. During this time, there was evidence of double standards being applied on account of the archbishop's possible involvement in the then ongoing and unresolved John Smyth affair. In December 2020 I wrote another letter to the press as follows:

> *'Many people will be bemused that the National Safeguarding Team (NST) has cleared the Archbishop of Canterbury over allegations that he failed to act correctly in the John Smyth affair… The NST states that the claim against him has not been*

substantiated. Does this mean that the Archbishop is innocent? Or does it mean, as in the case of a certain illustrious late Bishop of Chichester, that, in Archbishop Welby's own words, a "significant cloud" remains over his reputation?' (Church Times, 11 December 2020)

It would appear from the Makin report into this affair, published five years late on 7 November 2024, that the archbishop did indeed 'fail to act correctly'. The findings of this report also certainly seem to indicate that the National Safeguarding Team came to the wrong conclusion four years ago. It should, of course, be borne in mind that the NST is not an independent body itself, being comprised either of Church representatives or those appointed by the Church.

However that may be, Welby was not alone in his ambivalence in the George Bell case. Undoubtedly taking their cue from the fence-sitting of some senior church leaders involved, others have also been very slow to accept that a single unsubstantiated allegation is not a basis on which to condemn a man and traduce his reputation out of hand, as will be shown in the next chapter. There is no reason now not to set the record straight. James had written to both Archbishop Welby and to Bishop Warner on 6 February 2019, saying *'You cannot destroy a person's reputation, and then say, "Well, we didn't get our processes right".'* This excerpt from Bishop Warner's response to him indicates the ongoing reluctance of some to acknowledge the fundamental miscarriage of justice that had been perpetrated:

> 'Publication of an allegation and our response to it... has inevitably been read as a statement that breaches the presumption of innocence. As we do acknowledge, this was wrong.' But he continues: 'We cannot now unpublish that information or turn the clock back'. (25 February 2019)

On the contrary, it most certainly can be 'unpublished'. The clock can still be turned back with a public statement acknowledging the miscarriage of justice that has occurred, and with the prompt and complete restitution of George Bell's name and reputation throughout Chichester and elsewhere. Despite some recent progress and initial steps in this direction, elaborated below, there is still a considerable way to go.

CHAPTER SIX
Rocky Road to Restitution

An Epidemic of Ambivalence

EVEN BEFORE OCTOBER 2015, I was interested in the possibility of creating a memorial fund or project in George Bell's name to work with refugees. The events of the preceding summer that precipitated the Syrian refugee crisis had caused me to write in early September 2015 to a local senior church official, asking who among the present church leadership was taking a proactive stance on the situation in both political and ecclesiastical circles, as I maintained Bishop Bell would have done. I was dismayed by my contact's response. Until then, he had never heard of Bell. Sadly, a few weeks later, he had heard of him – but for all the wrong reasons.

Nevertheless I was determined to pursue the idea of a living memorial to the late bishop that would benefit refugees, whether in this country or elsewhere. I was certain that Bell himself would have wanted this, and had he been alive would in all probability have initiated and taken the lead in such work, attacks on his reputation notwithstanding. It was not just a desire for better worldwide ecumenical relations, but a determination to address the 'life or death' issue of refugees and displaced persons particularly in post-war Europe, that was part of the impetus for his involvement with the nascent international movement leading to the foundation of the World Council of Churches in 1948 and his own presidency thereof for most of the following decade.

There followed, for me, several years of frustration. There was a disappointing response from a number of potential partner organisations whom I approached with a view to co-founding a memorial fund or project for refugees in George Bell's name. Here are a few examples, chiefly from the years following the Carlile Report of

2017 and the Briden Report the next year, both of which had exonerated Bell:

One individual (August 2021) emailed to say: '*While we are always keen to support charities that help refugees… our trustees would not be prepared to set up a fund in the name of Bishop Bell.*' It was not clear from this whether he had actually approached the aforesaid trustees, or simply made the decision himself. From the speed of his response to me, I suspect the latter.

A year before that (August 2020), a senior cleric in a church that had seemed to be an obvious partner for a refugee initiative had written as follows:

> '*…we could not begin a new initiative under George Bell's name… as you know he now lies in a region somewhere between being branded with something and being cleared of something. It's a distressing situation for all who care about his reputation and legacy. But the church has a terrible record of dealing sensitively and appropriately with survivors, and in this generation it has to be especially mindful of the attitudes of survivors, individually and collectively. If it were an already-existing initiative it might be different. But to begin an initiative in this climate with this name would not be something [this church] would be able to do. I'm very well aware that many feel a great injustice has been done to George Bell's good name. But pursuing that cause through the establishment of an initiative like this is not something we could currently support.*'

I replied:

> '*I fear that I would not work well or comfortably with an organisation in which the fundamental presumption of innocence is not universally applied. I cannot accept that the reputation of the late Bishop George Bell "now lies in a region somewhere between being branded with something and being cleared of something". The single allegation of abuse brought posthumously against him has been shown to be unsubstantiated. The Church has apologised for the way in which it handled the case, and Archbishop Welby, at the start of 2019, welcomed the proposal for work on a statue commemorating Bell as Dean*

CHAPTER SIX Rocky Road to Restitution

of Canterbury to be continued.

> 'Working with asylum seekers and refugees of necessity entails working with many who have fled injustice in their own countries. It would be ironic for them to find themselves being supported by an institution that is not fully committed to the pursuit of justice here.'

This was not the end. The CEO of another organisation working with refugees expressed concern that potential *"reputational harm" to [that organisation] featured as a strong worry [among trustees] with others asking pointedly how we could be sure that it was not being used'*.

There was an attempt at a perhaps more subtle reply from another vicar of a church working with refugees, although he maintained (rather to my surprise and scepticism) that there was no need for extra funds at that point for a project which might have both reflected George Bell's own concerns and benefited itself from a further fundraising drive:

> 'I'm glad the work we are doing.... has permeated through to you and it has been good to remind people of the connection with Bishop Bell. What has happened since his death is so very sad.'

Indeed. Perhaps what has been saddest of all is that so many were ambivalent in their response, as these excerpts show. At least two others to whom I wrote never responded at all. One was a senior officer in a diocese that receives asylum seekers almost daily. Another was a representative of a national Christian organisation concerned with welcoming and integrating refugees to the UK.

It is worrying that so many public figures as well as private individuals still refused to accept and openly attest to Bell's innocence in the years following the Briden Report. It can be difficult for lay people to challenge church leaders, and sometimes even for such leaders to challenge each other. It is perhaps especially difficult in one of the smaller cities in the country, one which is dominated by its historic cathedral and where the ecclesiastical hierarchy is very prominent in local life. In a different setting, a greater degree of anonymity might have made it a little easier for some to express their concerns.

Continuing the Campaign

However, there were many who did speak out, or took decisive action in the George Bell affair. Both as individuals and as groups, people voiced their opinions in private and published correspondence and articles, in personal or collective submissions to the Carlile investigation, in meetings, and in other ways. We have amassed numerous names from letters, articles and various press clippings in our own personal files. Some of those involved are public figures and are perhaps more familiar names than others, but there are many people who, in various ways, have played a part in bringing about justice for George Bell. Every single letter from every single individual will have made a difference here. The fact that the case is still cited in occasional press excerpts demonstrates that even now the issue has not gone away. The list includes not just those who have personal or professional connections with the late Bishop, but people who – even if they did not know him at all – were sufficiently incensed by the injustice of the case that they were moved to write to the press about it, whether just once or several times. As already mentioned, it includes lawyers and judges, politicians, journalists, clergy, academics, and many private individuals as well.

This illustrates that the overall campaign was pursued not as a single organised movement but on a number of different fronts. Sometimes they overlapped, but more often they were pursued separately by different people. Two journalists in particular, Charles Moore and Peter Hitchens, were assiduous in their writings on the subject. Letters referring to the case, written by innumerable people, continued to be published in the papers.

There were also several collective efforts. The key role of the George Bell Group, and particularly of its convener Andrew Chandler and legal expert Desmond Browne KC, has already been mentioned. At the same time, a separate campaign was being led by Richard Symonds. In addition to his own prolific letter-writing, he organised a series of meetings in London and in Chichester under the 'Rebuilding Bridges' title (www.rebuildingbridges.org), with a wide variety of invited speakers. The series was concerned not only with the George Bell case but with other relevant issues, as well as with concerns of the late bishop himself.

Even before this, Peter and Marilyn Billingham, now both sadly

CHAPTER SIX Rocky Road to Restitution

deceased, had started a local campaign in Chichester itself. They were the first to begin leafleting outside the cathedral when the Church's decision was initially announced in October 2015. They continued their campaign by organising several meetings in Chichester on or around the late bishop's birthday (4 February), or the anniversary of his death (3 October). These brought a wider group of supporters together to encourage each other and to hear and participate in readings relevant to Bell's wide-ranging work and interests. Simultaneously, for several years running, Andrew Chandler organised services in London on George Bell Day, which were open to the general public as well as to invited guests.

Public petitions also played their part. In the late summer and early autumn of 2016, as noted before, Richard Symonds had organised a petition to have the case reopened in order to allow a defence to be heard. It attracted over 2000 signatures and was presented at Lambeth Palace in October that year. Later, in the spring of 2019, the late Peter Billingham organised a different petition with over 1000 signatures, calling for the reinstatement of George Bell's name on the front door of the house dedicated to him: 4 Canon Lane in Chichester. This was accompanied by a demonstration and leafleting outside that building on the occasion of the AGM of Friends of Chichester Cathedral in June 2019. Neither petition elicited a response at the time (Peter actually had a meeting with the incumbent Dean in person, to no avail), but both indubitably played their part in keeping up the pressure on the relevant authorities.

Whether separately or collectively, each aspect of the campaign was a factor in keeping the case alive and in its eventual, if still incomplete, resolution. I hesitate to name other individuals for fear of leaving anyone out, or of giving undue credit to one person at the expense of others. Suffice it to say that significant numbers of people were involved at various different levels and at different times, whether working collectively or as individuals. The present work, for logistical reasons, can mention only a few by name. But all have had their effect, along with the legal submissions and supporting documents made to the relevant authorities. Archbishop Welby's retraction statement of 17 November 2021 recognises this:

'I apologise for the hurt that my refusal to retract that ['significant cloud'] statement has caused to Bishop Bell's surviving relatives, colleagues and longstanding supporters. They have all

raised this issue, often powerfully, and I have recognised my error as a result of their advocacy.'

More will be said about this statement below.

By contrast, there was a complete dearth of published material in support of the Church's actions. And the single published letter that I have found did nothing to substantiate any case against Bell. On the contrary, it could be taken as an attempt to absolve those involved in the procedure from any further responsibility in the matter. It appeared just before the publication of the Carlile Report:

> *'If the allegations are false, and we apologise, we do an injustice to the name of someone who has died, but do no further harm: the deceased has been entrusted to the Father... If the allegations are true, and we fail to apologise, we do a grievous injustice... This will have lasting consequences on the life of this person and will make the Church an agent of harm'* (The Rev Tom Brazier, Church Times, 10 November 2017)

To which I responded:

> *'...none of [George Bell's supporters] would endorse the statement that "no further harm" has been done to the reputation and legacy of one of the country's greatest bishops. I would suggest that Mr Brazier visit Chichester and find out for himself just how much harm has been done... To support a potential miscarriage of justice in this or any other case on the grounds that the deceased is already "entrusted to the Father" beggars belief'.* (Church Times, 17 November 2017).

The possibility of a miscarriage of justice was one of the most potent arguments in favour of abolishing the death penalty in this country more than half a century ago. It is hard to imagine that the words of this particular vicar would have been much consolation to the families of the many people falsely accused and subsequently executed in years gone by for crimes they had not committed. And it is wrong to say that there are no 'lasting consequences' resulting from the false accusation even of a person long deceased. The trashing of that individual's name and reputation is immensely damaging not only to his or her living relatives and friends, but to the pursuit of justice as well as to historical fact.

Some individuals found other ways of demonstrating their belief in George Bell's innocence. Lord Lexden set an example in September 2021 when he resigned from the Parliamentary Ecclesiastical Committee over the Church's handling of safeguarding and quoting the George Bell case as a glaring instance of this. Voting with one's feet can often be a very effective means of protest.

Voting with one's money can help too. An example was set by Christopher Hoare in 2018, in his announcement that *'the £50,000 I had left to Chichester Cathedral will not be forthcoming until a building, now known as 4 Canon Lane, has its name restored to George Bell House'* (*Daily Telegraph*, 26 January 2018). Money speaks loudly, especially in the present economic climate. Meanwhile, every day that still passes without the complete restoration of George Bell's good name and reputation further undermines the presumption of innocence which is the basis of justice in this country.

Everything ground to a halt with the outbreak of the Covid-19 pandemic in early 2020. For a while, it looked as if nothing more could be done, in the shorter term at least.

At last! Light at the End of the Tunnel

However, the campaign to initiate a refugee project in memory of the late Bishop eventually achieved a successful outcome, pandemic notwithstanding. In September 2021 I was introduced by Lord Carey of Clifton, former archbishop of Canterbury, to The Rev Dr Patrick Sookhdeo, then director of Barnabas Aid. The latter immediately and unequivocally expressed his support for the idea of a specifically named Bishop George Bell Memorial Fund supporting convert leadership among persecuted Christians. This was very much in line with Bell's own support for non-Aryan pastors fleeing the Nazi regime (such as my father) in the late 1930s and early 1940s. I learned that the work and example of the late Bishop had been integral to the founding of the charity in the 1990s. At last, it was a meeting of minds.

We opened the Bishop George Bell Memorial Fund through Barnabas Aid that same month and formally launched it at events in both London and Chichester in early February 2022. Lord Carlile was the keynote speaker at the London event on 3 February, in what became the first in a new series of George Bell Memorial Lectures. In response to a direct question by the journalist Peter Hitchens (well known for his numerous columns in defence of Bell in the *Mail On Sunday*), Lord Carlile publicly declared that Bell was not guilty, reaffirming the findings of his 2017 report. There had never been a case against him.

I am grateful to Lord Carey and to staff at Barnabas for their active support in initiating and promoting the Fund from the outset. Despite some current problems within the organisation (relating not to its work but to its governance), the Fund has already saved the lives of several pastors in Africa and Asia and supported a number of their families. Separately, Lord Carey obtained funding from a generous donor to continue a regular George Bell Memorial Lecture series. The second lecture was given by Lord Alton at Lambeth Palace, on genocide, in October 2023. Plans for subsequent lectures, featuring Bell's legacy in the present century, are currently ongoing.

So what further progress has been made toward restitution? In response to the inferred accusation in some quarters that I might have been attempting to use a memorial fund or refugee project for the purpose of gaining support for the George Bell campaign, I can honestly say that from the outset, that thought would never have even entered my head other than as a way of trying to encourage church leaders to be more outspoken and more proactive about the refugee situation than seemed to be the case at the time. The fact that the Syrian refugee crisis coincided with the Church's shock announcement about Bell's presumed guilt in October 2015 was entirely coincidental. It is true that the appalling way in which the George Bell case was being handled reinforced, rather than undermined, my determination, convinced as I was that this is something the late bishop would have wanted. And it is certainly a fact that since the Bishop George Bell Memorial Fund was first initiated in September 2021, there were almost immediately several positive moves in the direction of restitution. I am fully aware that other factors have also been at work here, in addition to the existence of the Fund itself. But the latter has certainly played a part, however small, in some of those developments.

The first of these positive moves was the already mentioned and long-awaited statement by Archbishop Welby, on 17 November 2021, retracting his infamous 'significant cloud' remark of almost four years previously. Against the background of a General Synod taking place in London at the time, Welby commented that

CHAPTER SIX Rocky Road to Restitution

> '*Previously I refused to retract that statement and I was wrong to do so. I took that view because of the importance we rightly place on listening to those who come forward with allegations of abuse, and the duty of care we owe to them. But we also owe a duty of care to those who are accused*'.

This statement was very welcome, even if it fell short of the hoped-for unreserved apology for making the remark in the first place. It demonstrates, as do several of the earlier quotations from Bishop Warner, that some of the most senior church leaders in this country feel very uncomfortable about speaking up for truth if this means appearing to take sides against someone who claims to have been abused – even if that claim is unfounded – by a member of the clergy. Nevertheless, Welby's statement can be taken as evidence that the collective pressure of support from so many individuals over so long a period had its effect in keeping the case alive, and that the former archbishop did belatedly, if indirectly, concede Bell's innocence. If he genuinely believed that the late bishop had been a paedophile, he surely would not have made it. It is a matter of great personal pleasure for me to be able to say that Archbishop Welby not only made a handsome contribution to the Memorial Fund, which was launched on that occasion, but also wrote a public endorsement as follows:

> '*I am so pleased this Memorial Fund will be able to honour the issues Bishop George Bell held so close to his heart and fought for throughout his life and ministry. Extending the light of Christ to those in darkness and the love of God to those who face persecution is a fitting way to uphold his pursuit of justice and peace for the most vulnerable, and the hope this work will provide to Christians around the world is immeasurable. My prayers remain with those who have worked so hard to set up this fund, and all who will be aided and comforted by its use.*' (March 2022)

Bishop Warner followed the Archbishop's example, making a generous donation from his personal funds, with the following endorsement:

> '*The creation of the Bishop George Bell Memorial Fund is a further testament to the fact that his work has withstood the*

test of time and is as relevant now as it was 80 years ago. I am delighted to support it'. (September 2022)

Would either of these two prominent senior clerics have contributed to a hypothetical Jimmy Savile memorial fund for sick children at Stoke Mandeville Hospital, however laudable the aims of such a fund? I doubt it. If the Bishop George Bell Memorial Fund gave them an indirect opportunity to admit that the late bishop was no paedophile, and to begin to find a way out of their self-imposed dilemma, so be it. That certainly was not part of the original intention, although it is also certainly a step in the right direction. One day, perhaps they will see their way to issuing a full and unequivocal apology for their part in the Church's response to the George Bell affair.

But Not the End of the Road

There remained other questions to be resolved. One was that of a statue of Bell at Canterbury Cathedral, to commemorate his time as Dean there from 1924 to 1929, prior to being appointed to the see of Chichester. The statue, on which work had already begun for a niche in the exterior wall of the building, had been commissioned by the former dean of Canterbury, Very Rev Robert Willis, who was an ardent admirer of Bell. However, it had all but been abandoned following the fateful verdict of the Core Group in Chichester in October 2015. But following the publication of the Carlile Report on 15 December 2017, references to the earlier plans for the statue began to appear in the press. Just over a year later, after the publication of the Briden Report, Peter Hitchens wrote to *The Guardian* asking: '*Has the time not come to recognise [Bishop Bell's] vindication?*' while the *Daily Telegraph* reported on 26 January 2019 that Canterbury Cathedral had announced that the planned statue would now be completed. Archbishop Welby issued a statement via Twitter affirming his support:

'I warmly welcome the announcement today that the statue of Bishop George Bell will in due course be completed and installed at Canterbury Cathedral, as a permanent reminder of his unique contribution to international peace and to the Church of England.'

More than five years later, in 2024, it appears that there has still been no progress on this. Dean Willis retired in 2022 and has subsequently died. However, in November 2021, in his statement regretting the delay in retracting his earlier 'significant cloud' remark, Justin Welby had repeated his hope that the project would come to fruition. *'Bishop Bell'*, he said,

> *'was and remains one of the most courageous, distinguished Anglican bishops of the past century, committed to the peace and hope of Jesus Christ in a time of conflict and war. The debt owed to him extends far beyond the Church that he served and is one that we share as a society. I am delighted that the statue to him that was planned will be erected on the west front of Canterbury Cathedral, where he served as a Canon, as soon as the extensive repair and maintenance works are complete.'*

But there had sadly been a complete lack of response from the former Dean of Canterbury Cathedral regarding progress on this front, despite the positive words noted above from Justin Welby in January 2019 welcoming the promised revival of the project. I myself wrote twice to the dean, in January 2020 and again in October that year, but received no reply. Other members of the George Bell Group, and several more individuals, reported the same experience.

Hopefully this may yet move forward, finances permitting. There can be no other acceptable reason for further delay. However, as of the time of publishing this book, no progress can yet be reported. In this instance, it is not so much a question of restitution, since no statue had been removed. Rather, it is a question of acknowledging the huge contribution to Canterbury Cathedral of one of its most eminent deans, and of ensuring that his memory is honoured in that building too.

The George Bell House Saga

Probably the single most important issue still to be resolved as late as the summer of 2023 was the restoration of George Bell's name to the front entrance of 4 Canon Lane in Chichester. A fundraising campaign from 2006 was specifically for a 'George Bell House: continuing the many passions of Bishop George Bell'. This building was dedicated to George Bell by former Archbishop Williams in October 2008. But Bell's name was peremptorily removed from the front entrance after the shock announcement of October 2015, and its restoration was a long time in coming.

Meanwhile, Dietrich Bonhoeffer's name remained on one of the rooms in that building. I often wonder how Bonhoeffer, a very close friend of my father and the person who initially introduced him to Bishop Bell, would have felt about this. On 31 October 2016, I wrote as follows to the Very Rev Stephen Waine, then Dean of Chichester Cathedral:

> '...Had it not been for Bishop Bell, Bonhoeffer would never have gone to Chichester... It was partly due to Bonhoeffer's influence that Bell played such a major role in drawing attention to the evils of Nazism, in assisting Jewish refugees to come to this country in the late 1930s and in helping them during the war...
>
> 'Without the connection to George Bell, the name Bonhoeffer would not appear in 4 Canon Lane. As the daughter of a very close friend of both Bell and Bonhoeffer, I request that it should be removed forthwith, unless the case is reopened or unless the name George Bell is restored.'

I received what I regarded as a very unsatisfactory reply to this letter, dated 9 November 2016, that

> 'I do not agree that a case can be made for removing the name of Dietrich Bonhoeffer from the room at 4 Canon Lane which is named after him. Bonhoeffer is a significant figure in his own right'.

I felt this completely missed the point. Accordingly, I wrote a follow-up letter on the same subject that was published several days later in the *Chichester Post* on 18 November 2016:

> 'I do not believe that [Bonhoeffer] would wish his name to be associated with a Diocese that has... engaged in a Nazi-style travesty of justice against his friend: proceedings carried out in secret and with no legal authority, sources not revealed, a defence not allowed nor even sought, a presumption of guilt and the consequent ruin of a fine reputation.'

I fear that Bonhoeffer might have felt the same way about the removal of Hans Feibusch's portrait of George Bell from a position of prominence in the church named after him (die Bonhoefferkirche) in Forest Hill, south London. My father, at whose instigation the church was named for his friend on the occasion of the opening of its new premises in 1958 (the former building had been bombed during the war), would have been furious. The last I have heard, from the present pastor of the church, is that the portrait is to be rehung in its former place, which is currently being refurbished.

The former Dean's statement that *'Bonhoeffer is a significant figure in his own right'*, while incontrovertible, completely ignored the connection between Bonhoeffer and Bell in regard to Chichester. Moreover, there is another room in that building that also reflects its connection with Bell: namely the Dresden Room. It was Bell's courageous speech in the House of Lords in February 1944 opposing the blanket bombing of German civilian centres such as Dresden that gave this room its name. I am not aware that there is a special connection between Dresden and Chichester, any more than there is between Bonhoeffer and Chichester, that could account for its name appearing on a doorway inside George Bell House, other than that originating through George Bell.

I believe that the 'silent majority' who attended the Annual General Meeting of Friends of Chichester Cathedral in June 2019 showed their true feelings by the loud and sustained applause to the question I posed to the Dean on that occasion regarding the group's position on restoring the name of George Bell House. It may have been technically correct to maintain, as was stated on that occasion by Dean Waine, that the Friends had 'no position' on this. I accept the point that they were not officially concerned with matters affecting that building, other than helping to raise funds for it or helping with some of the events held there. But the former chair of the Friends, currently its vice-chair, wrote in the national press that *'there was never any good reason to remove [George Bell's name from the building]'* (Graham Toole-Mackson, *The Times*, 3 April 2021). It should not be forgotten, either, that George Bell himself founded the Friends of the Cathedral early in his time there. The Friends may indeed have had 'no [official] position' regarding the name of the building. But it would also seem to be the case that their opinion as an organisation was never actually sought.

And notwithstanding that spontaneous demonstration of overt support, there was still no change in this situation three years further on. It was reported that at a Chapter meeting in the late spring of 2022, the matter was debated for over two hours. Eventually it was decided to leave things as they were because some of those present felt that not to do so would show disrespect, and lack of concern, for victims of sexual abuse.

However, an interim compromise solution, at least in the eyes of Chapter, seemed to indicate a tentative step in the right direction. This took the form of a new temporary panel inserted behind one of the front windows of the building that appeared during the winter of 2022, around the time of the launch of the George Bell Memorial Fund. The panel read:

> *'By the gift of the Community of the Servants of the Cross, this House was dedicated by the Archbishop of Canterbury on 5 October 2008 as a centre for vocation, education and reconciliation under the patronage of Bishop George Bell'.*

The building, known as the Old Archdeaconry, had been the property of the Diocese of Chichester and had not in fact been previously owned by the Community. But the surviving Sisters and trustees raised a very generous gift of £1.3 million, which made its purchase possible. The donation was negotiated by the cathedral dean at the time, the Very Rev Canon Nicholas Frayling.

The wording of the panel was yet another example of fence-sitting. It was odd, to say the least. George Bell was never a 'patron' of 4 Canon Lane (which was only acquired by the Cathedral 50 years after his death), nor of any of the activities listed here, although he was certainly a very active participant in them all, particularly in reconciliation. On 5 October 2008, Archbishop Williams opened the service dedicating the building to the memory of George Bell with these words:

> *'May the vision and tradition of Bishop George Bell be always honoured in this place.'*

The new panel may partly have been an attempt to pre-empt further protests from Bell supporters. It was a small but somewhat non-committal step in the right direction. However, the wording was ambiguous and, for most of us, it did not go nearly far enough. The fundraising leaflet which had preceded the eventual dedication of the building had read, clearly and unequivocally:

> *'The Dean & Chapter of Chichester Cathedral have conceived*

George Bell House as a place dedicated to many of the passions (including ecumenism, the arts, vocation, education, interfaith dialogue, peace and reconciliation) of Bishop George Bell'.

It could be that the strange wording in that new panel was an attempt to paraphrase this statement without actually using the words 'George Bell House'. Moreover, the only passion of which Bell could rightly have been called a 'patron' was the arts, which was not actually mentioned in this new panel, and for which (as far as I know) George Bell House had rarely been used in any event. And yet, George Bell was at least mentioned by name again, despite the panel's clumsy wording, on the exterior of 4 Canon Lane.

But the failure to restore the actual plaque with George Bell's name to the front entrance to the building from which it was hastily and unceremoniously removed following the October 2015 announcement by the Church of England continued to rankle with many, and continued to be the subject of correspondence in the local press in particular. Its prompt restoration by those who had removed it might well have been seen as a giant step toward to a public apology for the gross travesty of justice that had occurred. There were numerous letters to this effect over the years, especially in the local press, of which just one example may suffice:

'First steps could be to replace the dedication plaque commemorating the naming of 4 Canon Lane as George Bell House by Archbishop Rowan Williams in 2008, seeking to reverse all other decisions to airbrush Bishop Bell from the memory of the diocese...' (Marilyn Billingham, Chichester Observer, 25 November 2021).

Together with Justin Welby's statement regretting his failure to retract his 'significant cloud' remark sooner, the simultaneous restoration of the name plaque to its former position would probably have been regarded by most of the late Bishop's supporters as a successful outcome of the campaign to clear Bell's name. In the event, it took another two years for this to happen. And when it did, it was mainly thanks to the efforts of a number of individuals who had not been directly involved in the decision to remove it in the first place.

On George Bell Day (3 October) 2023, an Evensong service of commemoration was held at Chichester Cathedral, conducted by the Precentor at the time, The Rev Canon Dan Inman. The rededication of George Bell House at 4 Canon Lane immediately following the service was led by the interim Dean, The Rev Simon Holland. Both of these have subsequently moved to other positions, but they both achieved more in a relatively short time than could ever have been thought possible in those intervening years. All of us who have campaigned in any way for justice in the George Bell case owe them a huge debt of gratitude.

The eventual restoration of the name George Bell House in October 2023, eight long years after its initial removal, has undoubtedly gone a long way to bringing the case to a final satisfactory conclusion. But until complete restitution takes place, publicly and unequivocally supported by those who had done most to destroy the late bishop's reputation, speculation about the case is likely to continue. Other related questions meanwhile remain unanswered, and may consequently invite further investigation.

CONCLUSION

AMONG SUCH QUESTIONS, perhaps one predominates in my own mind. Judging by the way in which the case was handled, it appears that the relevant authorities actually *wanted* to find Bell guilty of the allegations against him. If this is so, then why?

Some possible explanations have already been offered. In the wake of so many proven cases of child sexual abuse among clergy generally and in the Diocese of Chichester in particular, this may have been regarded as a golden opportunity to demonstrate support for victims of such abuse. Following the Archiepiscopal Visitation to the diocese in the winter of 2012, it was rumoured that the Archbishop at the time, Most Rev Rowan Williams, delegated the newly appointed bishop the Rt Rev Martin Warner to 'clean Chichester up'. The timing of Bishop Warner's appointment preceded by a few months the complainant's request on 1 September 2012 to the Archbishop that her case against the late Bishop George Bell be reconsidered. The climate within the diocese was verging on toxic as regards complaints against the clergy, especially in the wake of the earlier reports already noted and after the publication of the interim report of the Visitation by Archbishop Williams in August 2012.

So the case against the late Bishop could have been regarded as one well worth pursuing. This would be thought to help cleanse the very tarnished image of the diocese with regard to clerical child sexual abuse. At the same time, it was an opportunity to justify the confidence of both outgoing and incoming archbishops that the diocese was now in safe hands. There can be little doubt that the scalp of George Bell would have been a highly ranked prize in this regard, one that would have enhanced the position not only of the diocese but of some of its most senior clergy in the eyes of the Establishment at the time.

Closely related to this was a desire on the part of those same Church officials to be seen to be 'politically correct'. Lord Carlile has noted that the Church of England was well motivated in its determination to do right by the complainant. However, the wider context of the growing #MeToo movement and of the many cases that had precipitated this needs to be noted as well. Both Justin Welby, then Archbishop of Canterbury, and John Sentamu, previously Archbishop of York, repeatedly apologised in public over recent years for the many proven cases of child sexual abuse that were brought to their attention. It is, of course, right that they should have done so, although whether merely apologising is enough remains an ongoing concern.

But there are many other victims, who rarely receive an apology. They are the ones who are wrongly accused of such abuse and whose lives are often ruined in consequence. It may have been felt that George Bell was a safe target in this respect. His life could not be ruined, since he had been dead for half a century. But while the damage to his reputation was evidently regarded as an expedient if perhaps regrettable outcome, those responsible had probably not reckoned on the extent, persistence and rationale of the ensuing backlash against the blatant miscarriage of justice that would eventually force them to backtrack on their initial stand. And it is not true that it does no harm to traduce the reputation of a person simply because he is dead. As Cassio comments in Shakespeare's *Othello*:

> 'Reputation, reputation, reputation! I have lost my reputation! I have lost the immortal part of myself, and what remains is bestial.' *(Othello, Act 2, Scene 3)*

Nothing has changed in that regard over the centuries. As His Honour Lord Parmoor wrote rather more recently than Shakespeare, with reference to the George Bell case as well as that of others including Sir Edward Heath and Lord Bramall:

> 'The allegation is published and the damage is done. They are innocent but their reputation is besmirched for ever' *(Daily Telegraph, 19 December 2017)*

There could be another reason for what appeared, to Bell supporters and to Lord Carlile as well, the 'rush to judgement' that he notes in his report (paragraph 18). There has always been the possibility of mistaken identity (as alluded to in Timothy Briden's remarks). We should acknowledge that initially, when 'Carol' repeated her earlier

CONCLUSION

allegation of the 1990s to Justin Welby and thence to Chichester, it was genuinely thought to be 'plausible' by the relevant authorities. Lord Carlile found that 'Carol' was both believable and convinced of her own story, although Prof Maden questioned the reliability of her memory over such a long period.

But following the Carlile report, it seemed as if further allegations were dredged up, however incredible some of them patently were, in what appeared to be a final desperate effort to prove that George Bell was guilty of a number of sexual offences. This desperation may have been attributable to the various other cases in the news at the time, casting doubt on the reputations of a number of eminent individuals. (In addition, the Channel 4 interview with Justin Welby, which showed the latter's connection with John Smyth, had taken place only a few months before the Carlile report was published. In hindsight, a possible reason for the refusal to allow a debate on the George Bell case to take place in the February 2018 General Synod may have been to deflect attention away from another example of a badly managed safeguarding case in the Church). But it may also have been because many people at many levels within the Church did genuinely believe that 'Carol' had been abused as a child. Indeed, many others, including myself, believed this as well.

But if the abuse was not carried out by Bell, then by whom? Various theories have been put forward by some individuals who are much more familiar with the local personalities of the time than I am. One or two of them do seem to be very plausible. And most sinister of all is the possibility that the Church might be covering for one of their own number – even someone who might still be alive, at least at the time that the complaint was made. A published letter by another correspondent raised this thought, and he was not alone:

> '...*if Bishop Bell is innocent, as circumstances suggest, and if "Carol" is truthful, as the Core Group assumes them* [sic] *to be, then clearly there must be somebody who has escaped any consequence of his actions.*' (A F Jesson, *Church Times*, 5 January 2018)

In view of the history of proven cases of abuse by clergy in the diocese, as well as elsewhere in the country, this is not as far-fetched as it may sound. Especially in the light of the newly published Makin report on the John Smyth affair, indicating that very senior clergy covered up their knowledge of Smyth's abuse, perhaps the possibility of another cover-up in the George Bell case would bear further investigation. The suggestion of mistaken identity that was put forward by some people, especially in the first year or so after the Church's 'presumption of guilt' announcement of October 2015, was never thoroughly followed up at the time by any appropriate authority.

To sum up these thoughts is the underlying fact that the Carlile review, which the Chichester diocesan authorities had themselves commissioned, was only to be concerned with *process*: the way in which they had handled the affair. This could be taken as implying that they were fully aware that the case, based as it originally was on a single uncorroborated allegation, was inherently weak. They did not want the case itself to be reopened, as they must have known full well that a competent legal expert would drive a coach and horses through it. Not only that, but it might have uncovered yet another abuser in their midst. By commissioning an eminent and highly regarded lawyer to carry out a review that was to be focused on procedure rather than substance, the hope may have been that this would divert attention away from the case itself. Thus, if any apology were needed, it could be centred on the process and not on the conclusions of the Core Group. This is indeed what happened. A number of apologies have been recorded for the way in which the case was handled. So far, to the best of my knowledge, not one has been offered from those responsible for the actual outcome.

It is a fact that many of us as individuals can find it hard to apologise when we are in the wrong. And it is even harder for a public institution, such as the Church, to do so: not just for fear of losing face, but perhaps also because of possible legal or financial repercussions. It is much easier to apologise for others' misdoings, especially those for which neither the individual nor the institution he or she represents could possibly be held responsible. Thus the apology is completely pointless and, of course, unactionable, while at the same time appearing as 'virtue signalling'. One example of this was instanced by Archbishop Welby's prostrating himself before the Amritsar shrine in 2019 by way of apologising for the massacre – by British troops, not by the Church – that took place there a hundred years earlier.

CONCLUSION

Another is that of apologising to Jews for their expulsion from this country in 1290. On 15 July 2021 I wrote a letter to *The Times*, asking why the Church of England felt it was

> *'necessary to repent of 13th century edicts against the Jews, when it was not in existence itself until the mid-16th century? It is right to express regret about such edicts, but it cannot apologise for something for which it was not responsible. It would be more fitting if senior clergy would admit their guilt in those situations for which they are responsible. Their mishandling of a child sex abuse allegation against the late Bishop George Bell is one example'.*

On 16 December 2017, the day after Lord Carlile's report was finally published, I wrote as follows to the *Daily Telegraph*:

> *'In our current "moral crisis" we should follow the example [George Bell] set in his call "for courage and confidence, for thinking of the needs of others, and for faith in God"'.*

Seven years later, are we any further on? The 'moral crisis' has deepened rather than abated in the interim; and the Church in general and some of its key leaders in particular must bear some responsibility for this. If it does not set an example through its own behaviour, then who will? As a correspondent to the '*i*' newspaper recently wrote with reference to the 2021 census finding that the number of Christians in England and Wales has now fallen below 50%:

> *'Followers of Jesus Christ may be reluctant to tick the Christian box due to the muddying of the waters in recent years. A Church that strives to conform to the culture, rather than shaping it, is hardly worth subscribing to'* ('*i*', 2 December 2022).

I have found it simultaneously depressing and salutary to write this little book. It has been depressing because in the course of examining over several years my accumulated correspondence, the same questions have been raised over and over again, have never been satisfactorily answered, and in consequence have never been completely resolved. I anticipated that this would be a lengthy work, based on the bulky file of material that we have accumulated over the past years. In fact, it has turned out to be much shorter than predicted – although doubtless this will be a relief to some of my readers, who will have found it more than long enough.

One reason for its brevity, indeed the main one, is the repetitious nature of so much of the correspondence. This has been tedious in the extreme to sort through. There has been a limit to the number of times I could repeat the 'presumption of innocence' principle in these pages, without boring both my readers and myself. This principle has been reiterated by so many people, so many times, in letters and columns in the press. And as previously indicated, I suspect that the lack of substantive responses by those in authority to whom letters were addressed on the subject was a deliberate tactic to stall the debate, in the hope that it would eventually be kicked into the long grass.

It has also been depressing because, despite the admission by the most senior clergy that 'Bell could not be found guilty', that the process of attempting to do so had been badly handled and had resulted in a gross miscarriage of justice, that the 'significant cloud over his name' remark has finally and publicly been corrected, and that the name George Bell House has now been reaffixed next to the door of 4 Canon Lane, full restitution has still not taken place. Nor can it be until an unequivocal public statement of Bell's innocence is issued by those concerned, and his name and image restored to all the various places from which they were peremptorily removed.

Yes, this will mean eating a large piece of humble pie. But surely those who lead worshippers in examining their consciences and exhorting their individual as well as collective repentance every day should be capable of setting an example by doing so themselves. In fact, this would be a genuine example of Christian leaders literally 'putting their money where their mouths are'. Such a gesture might ultimately benefit the Church as a whole far more than the current policy of adhering to political correctness and following secular social and cultural trends, as suggested by the letter to the 'i' quoted above.

However, writing this book has also been a salutary exercise from my perspective. There are encouraging signs that positive outcomes are beginning to emerge from this whole affair. As Joseph said to his brothers in Genesis 50:20, *'you intended to harm me, but God intended it all for good.'* New opportunities are opening for the late Bishop's legacy to be felt again in the present century. The launch of the Bishop George Bell Memorial Fund is one example of this. If the Fund saves one single life in Bell's memory, then he himself would probably have said that this whole miserable episode had been worthwhile. It is actually likely that a large number of lives may be saved, and many more supported in some way, through the Fund. And this is already happening. At the time of writing, the first grants have already been allocated from the Fund to help convert pastors and their families fleeing Afghanistan and other places of danger to safety in a third country. More such cases are expected to follow.

Moreover, with the start of the George Bell Memorial Lecture series at the launch event for the Fund in February 2022, there are further possibilities that Bell's legacy could help to inform and influence issues of both national and international concern. For example, while helping save and improve the lives of a specific group of refugees is rightly the sole objective of the Fund itself, advocating the need to address the worldwide refugee problem from a Christian, indeed possibly from an inter-faith perspective, may present new opportunities for its eventual solution. Such a solution has so far evaded politicians everywhere. Bell was beginning to develop an ecumenical approach through his role in the embryonic World Council of Churches in the post-war period. It is quite conceivable that he would be seeking to tackle the question through this agency or through a new, perhaps an inter-faith, body in our own times. The lecture series may have a role to play here.

Finally, I do not anticipate that what I have written in these pages will immediately reverse the still continuing trend toward a presumption of guilt that prevails in so many safeguarding cases, and the resulting erosion of trust that is developing in society at large and in the Church in particular. But maybe it will form a tiny part of the growing attempt to reverse these trends. If the George Bell case becomes a classic example of how *not* to handle a safeguarding complaint, then that too – perhaps ironically – will help to perpetuate his memory in years to come.

I would conclude by saying that it has never been my intention to belittle or attack the complainant. I sincerely hope that she has obtained, and may still be obtaining, whatever pastoral and other support she may need, both from the Church and from other sources. But if this work should ever fall into her hands, then I pray that she may begin to understand why there was such an outcry at the 'balance of probabilities' decision that was announced in October

2015, and why it was effectively challenged. I also pray that she may forgive me, as I believe George Bell would have forgiven her.

ABOUT THE AUTHOR

Ruth Grayson, herself an historian, is the older daughter of Franz Hildebrandt, a close friend of the late Bishop George Bell. Her family, together with many others, owes its existence to Bell's lifesaving work with and for refugees from Nazism during the Second World War.

The author of the Introduction, **Keith Clements**, is a widely published and internationally recognised Dietrich Bonhoeffer scholar who has also written on Bishop George Bell and other figures and topics. He is former General Secretary of the Conference of European Churches.

www.ingramcontent.com/pod-product-compliance
Lightning Source LLC
Chambersburg PA
CBHW060406080526
44583CB00012B/492